Books by Carl T. Rowan

South of Freedom
The Pitiful and the Proud
Go South to Sorrow
Wait Till Next Year
Just Between Us Blacks

JUST BETWEEN US BLACKS

Just Between Us Blacks

BY

CARL T. ROWAN

RANDOM HOUSE  NEW YORK

Library of Congress Cataloging in Publication Data

Rowan, Carl Thomas.
    Just between us Blacks.

1. Negroes—Social conditions—1964—Addresses, essays, lectures.   2. Negroes
—Economic conditions—Addresses, essays, lectures.   I. Title.
E185.86.R68   301.45′19′6073   74–9068
ISBN 0–394–47090–7

Manufactured in the United States of America

9   8   7   6   5   4

Acknowledgments

I am especially grateful to my journalistic colleagues, David M. Mazie, Genease E. Shivers and Susan E. Moore, for the writing and research and the immensely valuable insights that they have brought to these "Black Perspective" broadcasts and to the production of this book.

I am indebted also to J. Thomas Pride, vice president of Ross Roy, Inc., the advertising agency handling the Chrysler Corporation account. To Pride goes a tribute for pushing his belief that socially responsible corporations ought to sponsor programs designed to *lift* the level of life in Black America.

I wish also to thank Ross Roy for relinquishing its rights pertaining to these commentaries in order that they might become the heart of this book.

And I extend special gratitude to those radio station managers who have worked diligently to ensure that the "Black Perspective" broadcasts reached the widest possible segments of their audiences. It was the incredible response from their listeners that convinced all of us that these commentaries ought to be compiled as a book and made available to all Americans.

Dedicated to

Those unfortunate Americans who, cheated of education and deprived of opportunity, are generally victimized and exploited throughout their lives. May this book help them to discover that even a little learning can be a liberating thing.

Contents

Foreword

I kid myself, of course, in even pretending that this book can be a private dialogue between one uneasy and frequently angry black American and the millions more who languish out there somewhere between hopelessness and despair. In this era of Watergate venality and general intrigue, no man can speak even with his wife with total certainty that their utterances are private. Yet this book had its beginnings in one hundred radio commentaries in which one black man spoke as honestly as he knew how to other blacks about the hopes and horrors, the pains and promises, of being black in America in an era when power was in the hands of Richard Nixon, Spiro Agnew, John N. Mitchell, H. R. (Bob) Haldeman, John Ehrlichman and the rest of those wonderful people who brought us Watergate.

These commentaries are what I have said to the dwellers of fifty of our once-greatest, fastest-decaying cities about how to survive when the legal minimum wage is $1.60 an hour and hot dogs are $1.20 a pound and you discover that you aren't even protected by the minimum wage law. This book is full of black tête-à-têtes about illigitimate babies, and whether abortion means black genocide.

But I don't really mind a few whites eavesdropping

inside these pages. I know better than most Americans that for all the racial segregation and isolation that exist and persist in this troubled society, there is no separate black world to which anyone can speak exclusively. Nor is there any white world, however rich, arrogant, bigoted, that is not touched, or whose children will not be affected, by the issues and problems that are discussed in these essays.

If millions of black Americans were contemptuous of Agnew and his unctuous utterings about law-and-order in those days when society matrons paid more attention to him than did prosecutors, so were millions of white Americans.

So millions of black people shuddered when John Mitchell claimed the right to bug or wiretap any American he considered to be an "internal security threat"? Far more white Americans shivered at the suggestion—and breathed not too easily even when the Supreme Court ruled Mitchell's surveillance schemes unconstitutional.

So a lot of blacks felt that Watergate represented the greatest threat to this society's free institutions since Paul Revere shouted, "The Redcoats are coming"? Far more white people at least now recognize that a handful of arrogant men of police-state mentality resorted to crime, and came perilously close to turning this nation into a dictatorship.

All this is to say that the vast majority of these commentaries might just as properly have been beamed at white America. For as uninformed as black Americans are on far too many things, it is the ignorance of white America that feeds much of the trauma and tragedy of this society.

Can it be an accident that black Americans were saying that Richard Nixon was a menace, a man of less than honorable intent, long before white America began to clamor for his resignation or impeachment? This book documents a special perception and courage on the part of those outcast Americans who might have been most timid.

We are dealing here with social security, and whether the regressive tax that finances it is an outrage; and with drinking booze, of which many of us do too much, and black men outdo white men, and white women outdrink black women, for reasons I don't pretend to understand. We are talking about high blood pressure, a menace to everyone, but a special killer among blacks. And crime in the streets? What white American needs to know less about the facts than black Americans?

LISTEN, WHITE AMERICA! It wouldn't make much difference if I had given this book that title, for white America remains terribly nervous about black America. Maybe whites know that our destinies are hopelessly intertwined. They must figure by now that the Russians want to screw us all. The energy crisis does not recognize the color of an empty gas tank. Maybe drug peddlers used to prefer brunettes, but now they like blondes too—even in the once-sacrosanct precincts of suburbia.

It will surprise many readers, black and white, that the commentaries that make up this book originally were "Black Perspective" radio broadcasts sponsored by the Chrysler Corporation. Can you imagine that Chrysler *paid* me to say, and half a hundred stations to broadcast, remarks that might have caused unhappiness in the most powerful circles of government? Chrysler did.

I am still amused by the letter I received from an official of the Interreligious Foundation for Community Organization (IFCO) asking for copies of a commentary about the energy crisis. "It was unclear what your position is at Chrysler Corporation," she wrote, "and it seemed contradictory that your strong analysis of some of the ills of this system was afforded an airing by a major corporation."

It is on the one hand a new day in America, and on the other hand in keeping with the oldest traditions of this republic that Chrysler should say to me: "The time is yours; say what you believe your audience needs to hear."

But, then, what the hell? American corporations have been saying that to white journalists for generations!

Okay. Now you're asking *why* Chrysler did it. You're expecting me to tell you how many Darts, Valiants, Dusters and Imperials black people buy. The answer is: *I don't know.* To Chrysler's credit, no one there has ever asked *me* for proof that these commentaries cause blacks to buy Chrysler cars. I want to believe that someone at Chrysler decided that not even the fifth largest corporation in America could feel secure if 11 per cent of our citizens were lacking the information that is essential to good health, happiness and responsible citizenship. At Chrysler they understand—at least now— what I'm talking about when I refer to rats biting children at night, or youngsters dying from lead poisoning caused by eating paint that falls from apartment ceilings, or a ghetto dweller being ripped off by an energy-crisis crook who claims he has a gadget that will make a furnace burn twice as long on a gallon of oil.

The white reader will quickly realize, I hope, that while these commentaries are directed at black Americans, they are about an entire society that got caught up in a miasma of crime, greed, hatred, distrust—even as it was bereft of saving leadership.

CARL T. ROWAN

Washington, D.C.
March 1974

Part I

Black Perspectives on the Nixon Administration

Nothing matters more to blacks, or to any other people, than their status in society—their capacity to influence the government that determines their destiny.

Nothing is more dismaying than evidence that the system of justice does not work . . .

Black America has been in limbo for all the Nixon years, with no real hope of major new progress toward first-class citizenship. They have struggled mostly to prevent an Administration they regarded as hostile from erasing or eroding the fragile freedoms gained in a generation of protesting, suing, bleeding, dying . . .

1

One May day in 1972 Roy Wilkins, the long-time head of the National Association for the Advancement of Colored People, made this comment about President Nixon: "We thought he'd be President of all the people. Instead of that, he's with the enemies of little black children."

That bitter remark, by a black leader with no political ax to grind, says a lot about the civil rights record of the Nixon Administration.

Roy Wilkins was not the first moderate black leader to accuse Mr. Nixon of working against blacks. In 1970 Bishop Stephen G. Spottswood told the NAACP convention that "This is the first time since 1920 that the national administration has made it a matter of calculated policy to work against the needs and aspirations of the largest minority of its citizens."

Yet there are blacks campaigning for Mr. Nixon. They talk of winning 25 per cent of the black vote for the Republicans on the strength of Mr. Nixon's civil rights record.

What is the truth about the Nixon Administration and the black man?

Well, there once was a strong Civil Rights Division in the Department of Health, Education and Welfare. It's head, Leon Panetta, was ousted two years ago, in 1970. He named four of Mr. Nixon's top aides as enemies of integration.

Dr. James E. Allen was a distinguished educator who, as Commissioner of Education, wanted to move vigorously to integrate schools. He favored busing where it was necessary. Dr. Allen was blocked at every turn by the White House, and finally was kicked out.

There used to be something called the Philadelphia Plan. It was a scheme under which the pressure of government contracts was to be used to force unions to stop barring blacks. Contractors would be told that they had to have a certain number of blacks on jobs to qualify as fair employers. In this election year Mr. Nixon has waged a campaign against so-called "quotas" and the Philadelphia Plan is virtually dead.

The record is clear that not one significant pro—civil rights piece of legislation has been proposed or passed during the Nixon Administration. On the contrary, laws like the Voting Rights Act have been nullified by half-hearted enforcement.

There is not a single black Nixon appointee that blacks regard as having real power, or measurable influence on the President and his policies.

It is clear that on his civil rights record, Mr. Nixon is not going to win many black votes. What is not so clear is whether he really cares.

2

Every novelist wants to write the great American tragedy. Every moviemaker wants to put it on film. But the real American tragedy probably was outlined recently at the 1972 annual meeting of the National Association for the Advancement of Colored People.

NAACP leader Roy Wilkins told delegates that the black people of this country are under a state of "siege" launched by "the executive branch of the federal government." Never in this century has a responsible civil rights leader made so damning a statement about the President of the United States and the people around him.

For many generations white America said to black America: "Education is the answer." The implication was that if blacks went to school for a while, whites would consider treating them like citizens.

But Wilkins cited President Nixon's antibusing stance and other antidesegregation steps by the White House as evidence that the "Negro American community is under attack in public education." In short, education may be the answer, but Wilkins sees the government trying to prevent blacks from getting that education.

Then Wilkins turned to housing and what he called "the mortar fire of discrimination in shelter." This black leader was noting that the White House had put an eighteen-month freeze on most federally subsidized housing programs.

Was Wilkins expressing black paranoia in his condemnation of this decision? Not hardly. Observe that Representative Wright Patman, a white Texan, condemned it and vowed that "fight, and fight we will." Senator John Sparkman, a white Alabaman, said the White House decision was "in complete disregard of housing needs of the poor and ill-housed of the nation."

Then Wilkins turned to the vital issue of compliance with fair hiring provisions by those with government contracts. He noted that one reason so many blacks are jobless is that the government no longer insists on compliance.

Wilkins summed it up this way: "Black people are up against the wall, they are opposed by all the might of the Nixon Administration, which has repeatedly demonstrated it is not only against minorities but poor people in general."

That is a pretty stinging denunciation from a group that is far from radical . . . that in fact still uses terms like "colored people" and "Negroes" instead of the proud new term "black people."

Perhaps the saddest commentary of all about the current

prospects for black people was made at that NAACP meeting by Aaron Henry, president of the Mississippi chapter. "We used to be able to call Lyndon or John when things got bad," he said, referring to Presidents Johnson and Kennedy. "But now," Henry continued, "we've lost the White House and the Attorney General. And when Nixon appoints one member of the Supreme Court, we've lost that too."

That summarizes with painful accuracy the black outlook.

3

"Don't blacks give President Nixon credit for anything good in the field of civil rights?" I find that question in a lot of my mail these days. I also find a lot of propaganda from a group calling itself "Black Citizens for the Re-election of the President." This group claims that Mr. Nixon's work for blacks has been "outstanding, but overlooked."

Let's take a look at some of the President's good deeds. Mr. Nixon's supporters emphasize that there are twelve black generals and admirals today, the fall of 1972, whereas there were only two when he took over. The President deserves praise for making appointments that were desperately needed in a military being ripped apart by racial conflict. But blacks argue that a few showcase generals cannot obscure the fact that blacks still make up only 3.8 per cent of the officers in the Army, whereas they make up a whopping 14.8 per cent of the enlisted ranks.

Mr. Nixon promised early to help blacks develop profitable businesses. To his credit, he has emphasized federal deposits in black banks, and over $500 million in aid to minority businesses. But blacks complain that this aid has helped only a trifling few affluent blacks and done nothing to improve life for the black masses. Some minority banks are using their new deposits to buy safe government bonds rather than risk lending the money to black people.

And blacks are aware that these are token programs. The money bragged about is little more than what the government spends to bail out one single corporation—like Lockheed.

Then we are asked to applaud Mr. Nixon as the first President to ask for funds to fight sickle cell anemia, a blood ailment afflicting mostly blacks. Some blacks do applaud. But blacks also know that a lot of politics is wrapped around the sudden fascination with sickle cell anemia.

Summing up, most blacks give Mr. Nixon credit only for a few "trickle-down" token gestures toward the dignity of black people. Money for a few bankers and businessmen, joblessness for almost 10 per cent of blacks. Publicized appointments for a few blacks in government, but hanky-panky with construction unions that discriminate against blacks.

That group of blacks seeking to re-elect Mr. Nixon is bombarding the black community with slick pamphlets full of grandiose claims. But this reporter finds them met with slim applause and an awful lot of laughter.

As I began these "Black Perspective" broadcasts, anger toward and distrust of the national administration was the single most important issue in black America. Nothing added more venom to the feelings of black people than joblessness—than their belief that President Nixon had chosen them and the other poor in America to bear the great sacrifices made necessary by his ideological passion for fighting inflation ahead of unemployment, hunger, sickness.

The rift between the Administration and America's minorities was widened beyond repair when the President launched an attack on job "quotas." I dealt with that issue on the two following broadcasts:

4

President Nixon has banned special job quotas for minorities. The Civil Service Commission says there are no such quotas anyhow. But a lot of white people cling to the belief that the government has been giving the best jobs to blacks. They think private industry and the colleges are also giving blacks unfair advantages.

A white columnist recently applauded President Nixon for banning job quotas. This columnist reflected the thinking of millions of white Americans when he wrote the following:

"It has reached the point in many instances where a black of inferior qualifications is preferred to a white with superior ones. A black with a modest academic record can frequently take his choice of half a dozen prestigious colleges; a white with the same or better grades often will have to settle for a state university . . ."

You might get the impression that blacks are riding some golden gravy train. The facts just don't support any such notion.

The latest Civil Service Commission report shows that of all government jobs paying more than $20,000 per year, blacks hold a mere 2 per cent. But drop down to the messenger, janitor, menial categories. Blacks hold 25.4 per cent of these less desirable jobs.

Blacks are 11 per cent of the population. If you add in Mexican-Americans, Indians, Orientals, minorities make up about 20 per cent of the population. But they hold a mere 2.7 per cent of the top jobs in government.

The picture is roughly the same in private industry.

The Labor Department recently put computers to work to determine what happens to a white man and white woman, a black man and black woman, a nonblack minority male and female, entering the Department with the same qualifications and working five years.

The white male winds up earning $16,217 a year; the white female $14,484, or some $1,700 less. Next would come an Oriental, Chicano or Indian, earning $13,843. The black male would make only $12,872, or almost $4,000 less than his white counterpart. The black female would lag even further behind.

The Labor Department attributes these differences primarily to race and sex discrimination.

The little progress that has occurred where black jobs are concerned has resulted from bosses spelling out guidelines and goals. Where such goals do not exist, personnel people regard talk of *fair hiring* as just lip service to be ignored.

Mr. Nixon has wiped out the goals and guidelines. Now

minorities already cheated to a shameful degree can expect more grim years of discrimination.

5

If you're still fuming over talk of banning job quotas for minorities, your collar won't get a bit cooler when you hear about an upcoming court case. The Southern Poverty Law Center, headed by Julian Bond, is suing the federal government on charges that Uncle Sam discriminates in the hiring of blacks in Alabama.

The Poverty Law Center is run by liberal whites and blacks and headquartered in Montgomery, Alabama. It has presented some pretty striking evidence that if quotas are giving blacks a gravy train any place, it is surely not in Alabama.

The court complaint asserts that blacks make up more than 25 per cent of Alabama's population, but they hold less than 3 per cent of the white-collar federal jobs in that state.

The Justice Department, which must defend Uncle Sam, has 264 white-collar employees in Alabama. Only 11, or 4.2 per cent, are black. The Selective Service System has 139 employees in Alabama, and not one is black, the lawsuit alleges.

There are no black federal game wardens, no black FBI agents, no black "revenooers"—that is, alcohol and tobacco tax agents—in Alabama. Only 2 of 901 rural mail carriers are black.

Calling this situation a "shameful injustice," the Poverty

Law Center is asking the courts to set a 25 per cent black hiring ratio for federal employment in Alabama. Now, this would be a quota of the sort President Nixon has been deploring. Ironically, the Justice Department recently helped to establish just this kind of court precedent in Alabama. It urged the court to set a 25 per cent black hiring ratio for Alabama state troopers because the state had refused to hire a single black trooper in thirty-seven years.

Can the Nixon Administration now say that what was a proper court ruling against Alabama would be a wrong court decision against the federal government?

It goes without saying that a decent job with adequate pay is essential to the dignity of any man or woman. This lawsuit seeks to liberate tens of thousands of Alabama blacks from the indignity of poverty, or menial, low-paying drudgery.

Another truism of American life is that money is power. Blacks will remain powerless in Alabama and elsewhere until they get the jobs that pay the money that buys the education, the know-how, the sophistication required for real success in modern society.

This, then, is a lawsuit the whole nation ought to watch.

Yet when I began these broadcasts it was frighteningly obvious that more than black America was full of unease about President Nixon—and especially about the people who made up his palace guard.

Something called "Watergate" had crept into the vocabularies of just about every American who breathed. It was important that this nation's blacks,

her hungry and harassed, understand the importance of Watergate to them ...

6

At a party recently a group of blacks was discussing
what millions of Americans have talked about for months:
the Watergate scandals. "No point in us rapping about
Watergate," one young man exclaimed. "It's just a squabble
between the white politicians, and we ain't gonna be any
better off, no matter who wins."

That young man couldn't have been more wrong, for
the Watergate developments could produce some very welcome fallouts for black people.

The Watergate scandal is vastly different from all other
major scandals in our history because Watergate does not
flow from financial greed. The people most guilty in Watergate were not seeking to fatten their bank accounts; they
were seeking political power.

The men around President Nixon who masterminded
the political crimes known as Watergate were in many re-
spects political and social zealots. They were not content to
see Richard M. Nixon re-elected; they wanted a landslide
so overwhelming that they could easily construe it as a
mandate to wipe out Lyndon B. Johnson's Great Society,
John F. Kennedy's New Frontier and the Fair Deal and
New Deal of Harry Truman and Franklin D. Roosevelt. The
Eisenhower programs were even too "socialistic" for them.

The men who heaped Watergate upon the President

were the same men who told him to put G. Harrold Carswell on the Supreme Court. They told him to wipe out the war on poverty. They convinced the President to make law-and-order, welfare and busing great emotional issues.

The men who plotted the Watergate burglaries and espionage are the same men who convinced Mr. Nixon to veto the day-care bill that would have freed many poor mothers to take jobs; that he should veto the bill that would have created public-service jobs and eased the plight of tens of thousands of blacks who are unemployed.

The people forced to resign or who have been indicted in the Watergate mess are the people who were running roughshod over Congress in a naked grab for more presidential power. And it was painfully clear that the more power they grabbed, the more they used it to kill off opportunities, hopes, dreams, for America's minorities.

Noted Republicans like Senator Robert J. Dole of Kansas have openly blasted President Nixon's former aides as the most arrogant bunch of people he ever tried to deal with. The whole nation will gain—and most decidedly poor people and minorities—if the President replaces them with men and women with even a touch of humility and compassion.

So, for all its ugliness, Watergate does carry some blessings. It may have halted a clique that was trying to turn the social and racial clock back at least fifty years. And that has got to mean something to black people.

7

Wherever I go these days, people keep asking whether the Watergate scandal has any special meaning to black people. The answer is that it has very special importance to the futures of black Americans.

It is important to note that a frightening network of illegal spying and burglary was part of the broader Watergate scheme. Domestic groups like the Black Panthers and Weathermen were chief targets of this spying, but included was surveillance of civil rights leaders and just about anyone advocating liberal change in this country.

It is not just an oversight that no black government officials have been tarnished by the Watergate scandal. Watergate was a lily-white operation because the mentalities of those who perpetrated Watergate were fundamentally such that they believed only their white "elite" should be in on the big decisions. What bitter irony that they might have gotten away with everything but for the dutiful eye of an $80-a-week black night watchman!

The most critical question for blacks is what happens after Watergate. As of now—late 1973—some twenty of those hard-line conservative aides have been indicted or forced out of government. Will the new men around the President convince him to change his domestic programs so they show more compassion for the minorities, the poor, the disadvantaged who are so numerous in this society?

We will not know any real answers until the various Watergate trials and probes run their course. But just you remember that the fallout will be of critical importance to black people—well, to the entire nation.

And do not overlook the fact that Watergate was not the beginning of "Big Brother" electronic snooping in America—and it will not be the end. Yet Watergate may have alerted millions of Americans to the fact that their privacy was vanishing, and perhaps some vital freedoms with it.

8

Do you remember that period a few years ago, in 1969, when I had a warm feud going with J. Edgar Hoover? The late FBI Director was incensed over my columns about how he had bugged and wiretapped Dr. Martin Luther King, and had leaked dirt and innuendo to try to destroy the reputation of the great civil rights leader.

I was arguing that the use of Army gumshoes to spy on civilians and the proliferation of electronic eavesdropping were an assault on everybody's freedom. I said that this was the cutting edge of a police state. But millions of Americans were too upset by violence on campuses and in the streets to pay heed to my warnings. Well, in 1973 a Harris survey suggests that the public now has gotten the message.

More than half the people in America now believe that "things have become more repressive . . . in the past few years," according to a poll by Louis Harris. Take the burglarizing of the office of Daniel Ellsberg's psychiatrist, Dr. Lewis Fielding. Only 10 per cent find that acceptable, while 69 per cent of the people call it "unjustified and repressive."

We learned during the Watergate hearings that the White House hired private detectives to spy on the sex life, drinking habits and family problems of political opponents. The Harris survey found that 83 per cent of the American people oppose these tactics, with only 8 per cent approving.

Three years ago the public was almost dead evenly divided on whether the Kent State shootings were "necessary and justified."

Then there's that celebrated "enemies list" that was drawn up in the White House. Harris reported that a whopping 68 per cent of the people now feel that the Administration went beyond acceptable bounds in drawing up such a list, and only 17 per cent find this practice acceptable.

The simple fact is that this society has come a long way from the days, only a few years ago, when American women felt that student protesters were the greatest threat to the nation—after the Communist party.

We have come a long way from the days when "civil rights demonstrators" were perceived to be among the most "subversive" forces in the nation. Millions of Americans who once were willing to surrender basic liberties if government would just guarantee a little tranquillity have begun to have second thoughts. They want some curbs put on government.

But what would the reaction be if we had a new outbreak of campus upheaval and violence in city streets? The majority probably would once again decide to accept government repression if it gave them a measure of tranquillity.

The Nixon forces defeated the Democrats because they had sensed better the vulnerability of the American people. They were not timid about appealing to the worst instincts of the masses.

"Job quotas," law-and-order, scare stories about threats to "national security," attacks on "welfare bums" . . . It seemed to millions of black Americans that this Administration had so vilified them as to alter public opinion in this nation—to make it newly hostile to the weakest people in the land . . .

9

The New York City Human Rights Commission has issued a very disturbing report about increased racial violence in that city. It said there has been an alarming upsurge of arson and vandalism against the homes and churches of minority families located in previously all-white neighborhoods.

The rights commission expresses fear that continued integration in the North will be resisted as forcefully and violently as it was in the South a generation ago.

The rights commission says that in some communities, fear merchants have whipped white residents into a state of hysteria over the mere rumor that a minority family is moving in. In Rosedale, investigators found, when two white families are feuding, the ultimate threat that one neighbor can hurl is: "I'm going to sell my house to blacks."

In one case, when it was rumored that the contractor

was about to sell a $53,000 duplex to nonwhites, residents of Rosedale took axes and picks and virtually destroyed the house while some two hundred other residents watched and cheered.

In the Forest Hills area, a fire described by police as "of suspicious origin" destroyed a Christian Assembly church whose membership was two-thirds white and one-third black and Puerto Rican. Police arrested three teen-agers on suspicion that they had set the fire in anger because they had lost their meeting place for drugs sessions when the building was turned into a church. Police said they saw no racial implications, but the church people noted that "Niggers get out" and swastika signs were scrawled on the building by the arsonists.

There is grim irony in another case of violence where white men in Ozone Park attacked a school bus and poured oil on black and Puerto Rican students being brought into the white middle-class school.

Violence is used to prevent integration through busing with the argument that children should go to school in their neighborhood. Then violence is used to ensure that no minorities can live in certain neighborhoods.

The commission suggests that violence in New York is typical of a racist upsurge in many cities. There is evidence to support this contention.

The question is how to halt this trend toward racial violence. The commission notes that violence was rampant in the South until there was vigorous action by local police and the FBI, and stern prosecution of the offenders. And so it will be in the North.

But hostility to blacks seeking homes, or jobs, or a hospital bed, or courtroom justice, is not new in America. What was new was *hope*—the hope engendered in a hundred Supreme Court decisions against Jim Crow, and Lyndon Johnson telling a joint session of Congress, "We shall overcome," and Congress opening up motels in Mississippi and voting booths in Alabama, and Sarge Shriver waging war on poverty.

Probably nothing soured the Nixon years for America's minorities more than the mostly overt but often sleazy efforts by the Nixon people to wipe out all the programs that gave hope to the hopeless.

Antipoverty, antisegregation in schools—there weren't many fighters for these causes close to this President . . .

10

Practically all Americans now know that the Nixon Administration is dismantling the Office of Economic Opportunity, the nerve center of the war on poverty. But my conversations around the country indicate that few blacks really understand what this will mean to them.

Until Howard Phillips, a founder of the right-wing Young Americans for Freedom, started busting up OEO, there were 906 local community-action agencies operating at a cost of $300 million a year. At the start of 1973 these agencies employed 184,000 people at an average salary of about $5,200 a year.

It is important to remember that half these people were living in poverty before they were hired for community action. When they lose their jobs, many will lapse back into poverty, go on welfare. So the public is being misled by Administration claims that "the money was going for salaries and not going to the poor." In half the cases the salaried workers are the poor.

To understand fully why people like Phillips dislike the community-action agencies, you must understand some of the things the agencies were doing. Outreach workers got millions of aged people enrolled in Medicare who otherwise never would have known their rights. That made Medicare a great human success. But archconservatives like Phillips don't want that much success, because it increases Medicare costs.

Similarly, there was a time when only 40 per cent of eligible people were getting surplus-food commodities, and only 20 per cent of those eligible were getting food stamps. Community-action people made the rounds, urging hundreds of thousands more to get the help to which they were entitled. And that wasn't popular with people more interested in holding down the budget than fighting hunger.

There were 207 agencies in forty-six states that were deeply involved in consumer protection, in halting the exploitation of the poor. And that was unpopular among the influential exploiters.

The federal budget for community-action agencies is being cut to around $100 million for fiscal 1974. After that, if local governments won't fund the agencies, they will die.

In communities with liberal leadership, the agencies will

get funds. In conservative communities, they will die. As for those towns and cities in the political middle, it will depend pretty much on how vocal black people and poor people become in demanding community action.

11

From the start of 1973 a storm has raged across America because President Nixon is dismantling the Office of Economic Opportunity. Dozens of congressmen have cried "shame" and "inhumane" as they sought to save the war on poverty. But Mr. Nixon argued that too much federal money has been going to those who were supposed to help the needy and not enough to the needy themselves.

Just what is the truth about these poverty programs?

When John F. Kennedy was elected President in 1960, almost 40 million Americans lived in poverty. More than 28 million of these poor people were white, and 11.5 million of them were black or other minorities. Or to put it another way, a whopping 8.242 million families were impoverished.

When Richard Nixon was elected in 1968, the Kennedy and Johnson administrations had reduced poverty dramatically. The Census Bureau says that in eight years they had lifted 3.2 million families out of poverty. That is, some 11 million white people and 3.5 million blacks had been helped out of degradation and despair.

How, then, you ask, could President Nixon kill the antipoverty program with the argument that it has been "a dismal failure," to use his words?

One answer is that the programs *have* appeared to fail since Mr. Nixon took office. The Census Bureau says that in 1971, the last year for which figures are available, more people were living in poverty than in 1968.

Mr. Nixon's anti-inflation policies produced high unemployment. Add to that his vetoes of public-works programs and you get an upsurge of people living in want and misery. The problem became even more acute as this Administration gave half-hearted support to, or even sabotaged, programs designed to help the poor.

Mr. Nixon speaks the truth when he says that not enough of the money was getting to the poor. The poverty programs did create a new bureaucracy of well-paid poverty workers. But do not underestimate the importance of this. Minorities got a lot of these jobs and they helped to create a real black middle-class. A lot of the benefits did "trickle down," as is evidenced by the 14.5 million people who rose out of poverty in the Kennedy and Johnson years.

There has been waste, corruption, inefficiency in the poverty programs, but no more than in most other government programs—no more than in many of America's big corporations.

This antipoverty fight is not over "waste" or the alleged "failure" of OEO. The problem is that Mr. Nixon's key advisers don't want to spend federal money on the poor, and they are going to reduce outlays as much as Congress and the public will permit.

The immediate outlook for America's poor people is simply an abundance of poverty.

12

It is hard to believe that more than nineteen years have passed since the Supreme Court outlawed racial segregation in public schools. In fact, so many minority-group children are still being Jim Crowed that they will not believe that the court ever ruled at all.

Let's take a look at some of the results of that historic decision known as *Brown vs. Board of Education.* The Department of Health, Education and Welfare will drown you in statistics showing that the old dual system of public education has been wiped out in this country. But the figures don't tell the whole truth. A lot more black children are in schools where there are whites. Blatant attempts to maintain "separate but equal" schools *are* generally a thing of the past. But the equality of educational opportunity that the Supreme Court mandated in 1954 is almost as far from reality today as it was nineteen years ago.

Take Prince Edward County, Virginia, a defendant in that original lawsuit. Whites there still operate a private "academy" so their children don't have to go to school with blacks. It is mostly whites who cannot afford the academy who send their children to the public schools.

Richmond, Virginia, is typical of what has happened North and South. Whites have fled to suburban Chesterfield and Enrico counties, leaving Richmond city schools predominantly black. They have used the technical barrier of jurisdictional boundaries to maintain separation, and the Supreme Court recently divided 4 to 4 on the question of whether the counties could be forced to merge schools with the black inner city.

Even where effective integration has taken place, blacks have been forced to pay a high price for it. The usual pattern of integration has been to destroy everything black and merge it into whatever was white. That made it easy to get rid of black principals and administrators, and fire thousands of black teachers.

It has taken years for the courts to face up to this injustice and require the retention of teachers on the basis of seniority. Where glaring racism has been manifest, courts have decreed that the black-and-white ratio of teachers must be the same as the racial ratio of the student body. Still, many thousands of dedicated black teachers have been ousted as the price for desegregation that the white bosses did not want.

Some blacks look at the pain, the bitterness, the trauma of the last nineteen years and they say that *Brown vs. Board of Education* wasn't worth all the misery it caused. So they talk about a reversion to the dual school system, or neighborhood control of schools. In the general frustration, all sorts of cowardly cop-outs are proposed.

But the truth is that that 1954 Supreme Court decision opened the door to fantastic changes in the South. Blacks live in infinitely greater dignity today. The humiliation and the physical danger are mostly gone. And children are better educated, better able to compete.

Still, we must struggle to see that the next nineteen years bring a lot more compliance with *Brown vs. Board of Education* than the last nineteen years have brought.

Richard Nixon and Spiro Agnew made the very most of their appeals to the fears, prejudices, hatreds of the great majority of Americans. By now millions of union members, farmers, housewives, teachers would probably like to forget that they gave the Nixon-Agnew ticket what appeared to be the clearest mandate in the nation's history.

But there was tragedy in the air. On "Black Perspectives" I talked about what Nixon-Agnew had done to the historic alliance between blacks and Jews—little realizing how soon I would be talking about what Agnew had done to himself.

13

Every American has his or her version of what was good or tragic about the recent presidential election campaign. In my view the most deplorable development of all was the split that developed between the Jews and the black people of America.

For more years than this reporter has lived, Jews and Negroes have been solid allies in the civil rights struggle in this country. It was a bond that grew out of mutual suffering. The Ku Klux Klansman that wanted to "hang a nigger" was also eager to tar and feather a Jew. It was a question of blacks and Jews hanging together . . . or hanging separately.

But a strange assortment of factors blended in 1972 to create an almost incredible picture of a few prominent Jews saying, "Let the blacks look out for themselves; we'll follow our own interests, which in 1972 means working for the re-election of Richard M. Nixon."

An example of this is Max M. Fisher, the Detroit industrialist, oilman and Jewish leader who visited most of the states in this country to raise money for the Nixon campaign. He was in Washington, D.C., in October 1972, urging an audience of seventy-one wealthy Jews to open their purses for Mr. Nixon. When someone asked him about the withering Jewish support for the aspirations of black people, the Washington *Post* quoted Fisher as saying: "Our interests are not parallel with those of blacks anymore."

This puzzling remark became clearer when Fisher cited Mr. Nixon's stand against quotas as a reason why Jews ought to vote for Nixon. Fisher raised the sad spectacle of Jews abandoning blacks crying for freedom the moment it appears that some college or business gives an opportunity to a black that might otherwise have gone to a Jew.

There is no need to talk about the selfishness of such a stance. The tragedy lies in the truth that the enemies of both blacks and Jews have managed to divide them . . . making it so much easier to oppress both.

Let me make it clear that Jews alone are not responsible for this foolish predicament. Some black militants have fostered it with anti-Semitic, anti-Israel rhetoric. Extreme black talk about quotas may well have provoked the American Jewish Committee into taking the public stand that Mr. Nixon exploited so shrewdly. Militant assaults on Jewish businessmen, some of whom deserved criticism, added to the malaise.

The election is over. And there is evidence aplenty that blacks and Jews have both been played for suckers.

Now that the passions of politicking are over, perhaps

both groups can return to the reality that their interests are just as parallel today as they were forty years ago.

But, as they say, "tempus fugits," and things change . . .

14

Spiro Agnew is no longer Vice-President of these United States. He left the office in disgrace, a felon convicted of tax evasion, accused by the Justice Department of his own party of a nauseating string of briberies and extortions.

The rapid rise of Agnew, the rash of criminality, the fall of Agnew, were all lily-white affairs involving hardly a single black person. Yet, the fall of Spiro Agnew carries lessons of the utmost importance.

It is no secret to any knowledgeable black American that the Nixon-Agnew years were not an era of great progress for minorities. It was a period of the "white backlash," of black people struggling to retain the precious gains made in the previous decade.

It was Agnew's pugnacious, sanctimonious rhetoric as much as anything that poisoned the minds of millions of whites and turned them against the black man's quest for equality. Agnew railed against "crime in the streets," sermonized in behalf of "law and order," in a way that suggested there was something racial about crime. Furthermore, his thinly veiled message to voters was: "Give power to Nixon and me and we'll put the uppity niggers back in their place."

Americans now know that Agnew was one of the biggest hypocrites ever to hold the second highest job in the land. While he inflamed the public against penny-ante crooks in the ghetto, Agnew himself was stealing the people blind. He and the Watergate crowd turned out to be the most lawless bunch ever to ride to power on cries of law-and-order.

Minorities need not gloat at the tragedy that has befallen the Agnew family. But they can hope that this society will now be drained of some of the ethnic poison that Agnew pumped into it.

But the optimism ought not get out of hand. This is still a society where people are more hostile toward a burglar who steals a TV set than toward a white-collar crook who takes $100,000 in bribes.

The Agnew case has dramatized something else for the public: that big shots get plea bargaining, fines and no prison term for major felonies, while the small fry gets locked up for long terms for stealing a loaf of bread. Maybe publicity about the Agnew case will push people toward a more even concept of justice.

The Agnew case is a disgrace to the nation. Obviously it is a costly way to teach Americans a lesson about phony political rhetoric and hypocritical justice. But the tragedy cannot be erased, so we had just as well learn something from it.

Part II

Black Perspectives
on National
Security

In war after war, blacks have fought for this country, yet discrimination remains rampant— even in the armed forces . . .

The nation has been warned repeatedly about the debilitating effects of pernicious racism, whether practiced by whites, as is traditional, or by blacks, which is a recent phenomenon.

In 1973 it became frightfully apparent (though millions of Americans would not see) that stupid racism and blatant injustices were rendering us a second-class power.

15

Racial discrimination and hostility are a terrible burden on this society. They cost this nation billions of dollars every year in lost production, social turmoil, physical destruction. But no segment of society views it with greater uneasiness than the military, where racial conflict has become a threat to national security.

During the last year, racial violence in the military has become about as commonplace as the Saturday-night crap game.

• In Korea, white GIs set fire to a gasoline soaked cross on a military base. Blacks retaliate by assaulting whites in the barracks.

• On Okinawa, a street fight between a white soldier and a black GI culminates in a bloody brawl involving 300 to 500 black and white soldiers.

• Forty-six men are injured in a series of fights aboard the aircraft carrier *Kitty Hawk*. All of the twenty-five men arrested and court-martialed are black.

• About 120 black sailors are put off the aircraft carrier *Constellation* when they refuse to go to duty stations because of what they say is racial discrimination and abuse, condoned by the ship's captain.

Hostility is so bad and morale so low in the military, largely because of racial conflict, that it would be a tragedy if the country had to fight a real war.

And now, with the country moving to an all-volunteer army, blacks are more important than ever to the military. The assumption has been that with the doors to economic equality largely closed to black men in civilian life, many would rush to the Army and Navy. There is a real question as to whether any able black men want to try a career in the military, with its growing reputation of unfairness.

The irony is that the ugly incidents increase and the military's reputation worsens at a time when top military leaders are demanding racial justice and fairness with a vigor never before known in this country.

In June 1972 General Michael S. Davison, commander of the U.S. Army in Europe, called all his commanders into conference to tell them that they were performing below standard in racial matters. In November 1972 Admiral Elmo R. Zumwalt, Chief of Naval Operations, was even more emphatic in berating a hundred top admirals and Marine Corps generals for inadequacy in carrying out his orders to improve racial justice and race relations.

Despite the integrity and the seriousness of Davison and Zumwalt, these men were trying to level the Rocky Mountains with a firecracker. One of Zumwalt's top aides, the Navy's chief of personnel, Admiral David H. Bagley, pointed out the difficulty of the situation when he said: "For hundreds of years there were few minorities in the Navy. We've been white-oriented. It's difficult to effect change overnight. Blacks historically have been stewards."

One clear thing is that blacks will never again be relegated to the role of sea-going flunkies. They are going to expect—no, demand—changes from this new, enlightened brand of military brass.

16

"I want to be treated like a man," cried the sailor from the U.S.S. *Constellation*. Black military men all over the world are saying the same thing. What does "being a man" mean to the black GI? It may mean finding some soul food in the base PX. Or being allowed to wear his hair Afro style. Or finding some rhythm and blues on the enlisted-men's-club jukebox, along with the country and Western music on which white cats groove. But most of all it means getting fair, decent job assignments; fair ratings and promotions; a fair shake from the machinery of military justice.

It was thirty years ago that I won an ensign's stripe and became one of the first fifteen black officers in the history of the U.S. Navy. They said a black lad wouldn't be welcome in the officers' wardroom aboard ship, or that a black officer could not command white sailors, many of whom came from the Deep South. They were wrong on both counts. One of my black colleagues in those pioneering days, Samuel Gravely, Jr., is now an admiral. He has skippered several ships and commanded a lot of white sailors over thirty years.

But the Navy is still pretty much a snooty, white institution. As of June 1973, only 5.8 per cent of its enlisted personnel were black, and a trifling seven tenths of 1 per cent of its officers were black. Until the Navy changes that ratio of black officers, black sailors are not going to believe they are getting a fair deal.

The Army is a little better. Blacks make up 14.8 per cent of the enlisted personnel, or more than the 11 per cent black ratio of the national population. But only 3.8 per cent of Army *officers* are black. What it means is that in Vietnam and elsewhere, blacks have carried a disproportionate burden of combat, of deaths, of injuries, of the heavy, dirty work. They resent it, and will go on resenting it, until major changes are made.

The Army has been setting up ROTC units at black colleges, so now close to 11 per cent of the officers produced in this program will be Negroes. On the whole, however, black promotions come slowly—except for the admittedly important showpiece promotions of blacks to colonel, general, admiral.

A black now sits on the military equivalent of the Supreme Court. The top brass knows that a black often receives harsh punishment for an offense that brings a wrist-slapping to a white GI. A top Navy official admitted that he was shocked and suspicious when a race riot on the *Kitty Hawk* led to the arrests only of twenty-five black soldiers.

Real justice is a long way from achievement in the military. Until it is achieved, our forces will be weak of spirit, and security will be in danger.

Yet, the military seems to be trying harder than the civilian leaders of American life . . .

17

You may have missed the fact that the Army recently promoted three black colonels to brigadier general. This item didn't even make some newspapers, and was mostly buried in others.

Wouldn't it be nice if newspapers could ignore these promotions because we had so many black officers of flag rank that it ceased to be news when a black man made admiral or general? We aren't there yet, so don't discount the importance of these latest promotions.

The new black generals are forty-three-year-old Charles C. Rogers of Indianapolis, forty-four-year-old Fred C. Sheffey of McKeesport, Pennsylvania, and forty-four-year-old Roscoe Robinson, Jr., of St. Louis. This means there are now, in the fall of 1973, twelve generals in the Army, three generals in the Air Force and one admiral in the Navy, my old branch of the service that always was a bit backward, racially speaking.

Anyone who cares about this country and its military strength must applaud these promotions. For, as I have reported earlier on "Black Perspectives," racial hostility and conflict have become grave problems in the military. Grave enough to constitute a national security threat.

An overriding problem has been the feeling of the black GIs, the grunts, the dock loaders, the cooks, that they were little more than cannon fodder, flunkies to be used and then abused by an unfair system of military justice. You can bet that that notion, realistic in most cases and paranoid in some, will persist as long as no black generals and admirals are in sight.

I know—some will argue that sixteen black generals and admirals still amount to tokenism. They can complain that the new promotions to general have little to do with the basic complaints of tens of thousands of black men at the lowest ranks.

Well, let me tell you a little story. When President Kennedy made me Deputy Assistant Secretary of State for Public Affairs in 1961, no black American had ever held so lofty a post in the State Department. You might have cursed it as tokenism, but it had impact throughout the Department. I'll never forget the day a black employee came in to tell me that he had tried for years to get a raise, but a white Southerner in the bureau always blocked him. That is, until the newspapers announced my appointment—meaning that I was now that Southerner's boss.

The prejudiced State Department officer quickly called the black employee in and said, "John, I've got good news for you. I just arranged for you to get a *double* promotion."

You can bet your last dollar that these new black generals will have their effect on the military system. They will be in a position to decide whether a lot of white colonels, majors, captains get promoted. And those colonels, majors and captains are going to think a little harder before they impose bigotry on the blacks who make up such a vital part of the enlisted ranks.

So let's lift a glass of something in congratulations to Generals Rogers, Sheffey and Robinson.

Anyone who thinks that the rest of the government, or private industry, can turn up a nose at the military need only consider the overall jobs plight of black Americans . . .

18

The Census Bureau recently gave us some good news and some bad news. First the good news: the number of poor people in America declined between 1971 and 1972. Now the bad news: the number of poor black people *increased* in that same period.

Of all the statistics compiled by the Census Bureau, probably none is more meaningful than those relating to family income, for the money a family has to spend tells an awful lot about the quality of life in that family. The Census Bureau reports that in 1972 the median income for white families was $11,549, but only $6,864 for the black family.

That means that for every $100 the white family has to buy food, clothing, medicine, shelter, education, the black family has only $59. That is a disturbing gap, for it is obvious that there can be no meaningful equality in this society when the economic disparities are so great.

But even more disturbing is the trend. In 1964, black families had only $54 for every $100 available to white families. Then, thanks to government programs and stronger efforts at justice by American business, the gap began to close. By 1971 the black family was spending $61 for every $100 spent by the white family. Now Census tells us that the gap is opening again, that the black family is falling further behind.

An especially disturbing aspect of the new Census Bureau report deals with the number of *children* living in poverty. For every 100 black children under age eighteen, about 43 live below the poverty line. That compares with 15 impoverished white children out of every 100 below the age of eighteen.

Think about it! The black child is almost three times as likely to live in poverty as the white child. Imagine how that increases the likelihood that a black child will steal something, or become trapped in delinquency. Think how less likely that average black child is to have newspapers, magazines, books, good records in his home. Think how much poorer the diet of that black child will be, how much less likely that black child is to finish high school or go to college. Small wonder that so many of the children on welfare are black. Census makes it clear that a vastly disproportionate number of our poor children are black.

There are a few rays of hope for black Americans in that census information. It shows that the black Americans enjoying the closest thing to equality are those just graduating from college. Firms are hiring them at salaries that are 97 to 98 per cent of what white graduates are being paid. This does not mean that they will get promotions and raises at the same speed as their white counterparts, but the black college graduate is being given something close to an equal start in that race we call the pursuit of happiness.

It suggests that every young black had better knock himself out to finish high school and get that college degree.

19

People who can afford to eat in restaurants used to contend that nothing was harder to attract than a waitress. In fact, a famous epitaph on a waitress' tombstone says: "GOD FINALLY CAUGHT HER EYE!"

These days, they say, waitresses are easy to get, compared with maids. Everyone pretends to want household help, and nobody admits to being able to find any. The fact is that 935,000 maids work in private homes, and they just might be the most cheated group of workers in this land.

The minimum-wage law was around before most of today's maids were old enough to swing a mop. It took a long time for Congress to decide that they need the same kind of protection as other workers. Maids are sort of taken for granted. Maybe it's because 97 per cent of them are women— or because 52 per cent are black.

Or maybe we've been indifferent because we never knew that two maids out of every three have children who depend on them for food, shelter, clothing. There are 275,000 maids in this country who are heads of households—and they have been working *full time* for less than $2,000 a year. That's about half the income needed to even reach the poverty line.

Recently the House of Representatives took an extraordinary step and voted to include maids under the protection of our minimum-wage laws. The House voted that maids must be paid a minimum of $1.80 an hour immediately with pay going up to $2.20 an hour in two years. Incredibly, the Nixon Administration opposed efforts to set a minimum wage for maids. President Nixon vetoed the entire bill.

But sanity has to prevail in this country at some time. Why should a man working in a factory with a wife and two children have more protection than a woman working in a home to support four children who are bereft of a father? The difference is that maids are not the most educated workers in America, so they have no powerful unions or lobbies. In truth, many don't know how to take advantage of rights they already have under the law.

Consider social security. Many employers don't know or care that a social security tax must be paid for any maid earning more than $50 in a three-month period. Many maids want to lose the advantages of social security because they feel they cannot afford to have their share of the tax taken from their meager paychecks.

It is crucial to the economic uplift of the black community that everyone take advantage of minimum-wage laws and other measures designed to guarantee fairness. A first rule of first-class citizenship is to find out what your rights are and then *use them.*

20

In September 1973 President Nixon vetoed another bill with almost life-and-death implications for the nation's poor people—which means, of course, that the veto is especially vital for black people. Mr. Nixon vetoed a measure that would have raised the pay of 3.8 million Americans by lifting the minimum wage from $1.60 an hour to $2 in November and $2.20 next July. The bill also would have extended minimum-wage protection for the first time to almost a million maids and household workers.

Mr. Nixon said the increase would be "inflationary" and that it would lead to greater unemployment of the poor, especially the black urban poor.

The Washington *Post* said Mr. Nixon's veto was "another shoddy attempt to blame inflation on an allegedly reckless Congress." The *Post* is correct. We have gone through four and a half years in which the Administration has fumbled with an assortment of phases, freezes, guidelines and other mumbo-jumbo that left a clear impression that it hadn't the foggiest notion of how to run an economy. It was strait-jacketing business with stupid controls—even while corporate profits leaped to a record $52.6 billion in 1972 and will probably hit $70 billion this year. It was saddling big unions with what appeared to be sharp limitations, while big labor still got away with murder in many circumstances.

The only people who constantly got hurt were the poor people, the little people, the minorities.

The bill that Mr. Nixon vetoed would have raised overall wages in this country 0.4 per cent, and this is of no significant impact on inflation. It defies explanation as to how Mr. Nixon could put the curse on this piddling sop for the poor when interest is at an all-time high and the cost of borrowing money has risen 62 per cent since January.

Baloney is now up to $1.62 a pound—more than an hour's pay for a worker at the minimum wage. And a President who earns $200,000 a year says it is "inflationary" to raise the minimum to $2 in November. Incredible!

Do you know that a person working for $1.60 an hour forty hours a week every week of the year would earn $3,320? That is almost a thousand dollars short of what the Labor Department says is the poverty level ($4,300) for a family of four. And even if Mr. Nixon had let the minimum go to $2.20, the annual pay would be only $4,576 a year, which is still pretty poor living in the richest country in the world.

Well, the objective is not to make you feel sorry for yourself. Black people do too much of that. The purpose is to make you understand that poor people get screwed because they rarely know the facts, and even more rarely do they rise up and sound off to the White House—and especially the Congress. If black people raised a little more hell with their congressmen, a lot more would vote to override a veto that is so patently unjust.

Well, I've given you some facts. I'll continue to do just that on "Black Persepectives." When you decide to get off your duffs and start looking out for yourselves and your children is up to you.

Part III

The Failures and Confusions of Blacks

So you figure by now that things haven't been going too well for poor people, or black people? And you ask why we blacks keep rushing forward and falling back?

One reason is that we are constantly losing the critical public relations contests . . .

21

Blacks keep asking me, "Where did the civil rights movement go wrong?"

My reply is that the movement is not what went wrong. Blacks simply have been outpropagandized these last few years. And they are not going to make any great new strides until they develop more clout in the field of communications.

Over the last few years there have been great public debates over law-and-order, busing to achieve racial balance, welfare costs, job quotas for minorities. In every instance, the debate wound up with black Americans cast as the villains. And this pointed up with bitter clarity the weak position blacks hold in the communications industry.

Are you aware that until a few years ago minority-group individuals owned fewer than 10 of the 8,000 or so radio stations in this country? Even today only some 30 stations are owned by blacks, Indians, Chicanos or other minorities.

The television situation is even worse. Black ownership is virtually nonexistent, and only one commercial television station has a black general manager. That one is in Jackson, Mississippi, where an interracial group took ownership after a license challenge. Seventy-seven per cent of commercial TV stations have only whites in any managerial job.

The Office of Communication of the United Church of Christ recently did a study of reports to the Federal Communications Commission by 609 TV stations. The study showed that 50 per cent employ no racial minorities as technicians, and 81 per cent hire only whites as sales personnel.

On only a handful of stations in America is a black free to give commentary on the top issues in the news. And almost nowhere does a black help decide what goes into the news, or into TV documentaries.

The situation is much the same on daily newspapers. The black who helps decide editorial policy is rare indeed. And there are only two or three black columnists who can sound off freely on a national basis.

One reason the Jewish people have fared well in this society is that they understand the value of communications. They know the dangers of being outpropagandized, so Jews have concentrated on the writing skill, on broadcasting, and publishing. We black people simply must train our children to write well, to speak articulately if not eloquently. That, too, is critical to the struggle for equality.

22

In April 1972 the Congressional Black Caucus sponsored a forum at Harvard University. A major subject was this country's radio and television stations, its newspapers, the rest of its communications media. The Black Caucus took the position that "There is widespread, long-standing and entrenched racism among the entire mass communications media all over the United States. Its policies and practices have had unfavorable and harmful effects on Black people and their institutions."

I support the Black Caucus allegation that ". . . the white establishment-controlled mass communications media has: (1) systematically excluded or exploited Black talent; (2) deliberately mishandled and distorted newsworthy events of the Black community; and (3) either ignored, played down or ridiculed significant efforts in the movement for Black liberation in America."

The Black Caucus concludes that "Television and radio are the most powerful and important forums of communication known to man." The Caucus was naturally disturbed, then, by evidence that this country's rulers are using the media to "obscure truths about racism, poverty, injustice, and economic and political repression."

If the Black Caucus is correct, the future is bleak, for 95 homes out of every 100 in this country have TV sets, and the majority of Americans depend on TV news for whatever comprehension they have of what is going on in this country and the world.

A black child watches TV an average of twenty-five hours per week, as compared with sixteen hours by whites. This, says the Black Caucus, "vividly illustrates the intensity with which Black self-hatred is reinforced by television's white-oriented programming."

This commentator has had an extremely rewarding career in communications. Yet I cannot dispute the Black Caucus contention that the media encourage blacks to hate themselves while they encourage whites to indulge in notions of superiority. But I do ask why the Black Caucus would stage that Harvard forum and then fade into impotent silence.

And listen to my next commentary. I'm going to tell it like it is about the failure of educated blacks to use the power they already have to influence and reshape the media.

23

A psychologist recently was complaining about the scarcity of black people in children's TV programs. She said youngsters see far more animals, clowns and goblins than they do black people—and that this is critical in terms of the ability of whites to think of blacks as human beings and normal Americans.

You know, from my last commentary, that some harsh criticism has been leveled at the mass communications media by the Congressional Black Caucus. But no one is saying much about *black delinquency* where radio, television and the press are concerned.

Most criticisms of the media by blacks are valid. We lost the propaganda battle on busing. Mr. Nixon carried the day propagandawise on the emotional issue of quotas. The black community became the culprit in all the hubbub over crime in the streets and law-and-order. Poor people and blacks came out on the dirty end of the public uproar over welfare. I have shouted for at least ten years that this is because almost no blacks are even *helping* to shape the editorial policies of the newspapers and TV stations in this country. Practically all those so-called black movies that are the current fad are dreamed up by whites, financed by whites, directed by whites—with the lion's share of the loot going to whites.

Blacks are *nowhere* when it comes to the media that shape public opinion. But what does the educated black American do? He sits around bitching over his beer in the expectation that some godfairy will suddenly produce a black Walter Cronkite, or some multimillionaire will leave a bag of money on the doorstep and say: "Here, produce your own black movies."

Forget it. Black people are not using the power they *have*. In every big city in this nation, black subscribers are vital to the daily newspapers. But have *you* ever telephoned or written your newspaper to ask why there are no blacks on the editorial-page staff? Or why your newspaper won't run—regularly—a black columnist who tells it like it is? When last did you or any of your friends telephone your newspaper editor, or television station, or write a letter to the editor about anything?

We blacks just must face the reality that progress comes

not from daydreaming, but from the zealous use of the powers we *already* have. Black David Brinkleys and Alfred Hitchcocks are not made in a day. But the power of the telephone or the typewriter can be exercised in minutes. The more blacks who *write* and *telephone* the media in their town, the sooner blacks will have stations and newspapers that are responsive to the needs and sensitivities of black people.

Another reason we gain three feet and lose a yard is that we talk "black power," but the people talking loudest often have no meaningful power and have no concept of how to get power, or when and where to use it . . .

24

A black federal judge, Damon J. Keith of Detroit, recently delivered a blockbuster ruling. He found the powerful, huge utility, Detroit Edison Co., and two unions guilty of systematic discrimination against blacks. Not only did Judge Keith order sweeping changes in hiring and promotion practices at Detroit Edison, but he ordered the defendants to pay $4.25 million in punitive damages. There are some vital lessons in this case for other major corporations—*and* for blacks grasping for the levers of power.

During brotherhood week several years ago in Minneapolis I went with the Urban League director to visit the head of a corporation that was hiring blacks only as janitors. When it was clear that this businessman was determined not to hire blacks in other categories, the Urban League chief chastised him.

"Don't you feel you are your brother's keeper?" he asked.

"Yes," said the company chief, "and a white man looks more like my brother than any Negro. That's why we give the good jobs to whites."

In this era of fair-employment legislation, not many company executives would utter such a brashly racist concept of "brotherhood." Yet the simple fact remains that racism influences hirings and promotions in all the major companies of America. This is so despite honest, zealous efforts by some presidents and boards of directors to wipe out invidious discrimination. The president may be enlightened, but the personnel manager or the shop foreman still figures that the white worker looks more like his brother.

Judge Keith lowered the judicial boom on Detroit Edison in the belief that only his unprecedented kind of decree could jar American industry out of the grip of entrenched, institutionalized racism. Detroit Edison has said it will appeal, and it may win relief from Judge Keith's ruling. Whatever the case, the message is clear that half-hearted attempts at corporate fairness in hiring and promotion will no longer satisfy the courts.

The lesson for blacks is that Judge Keith has shown what real power is all about. With a stroke of his pen on a monumental decree he has done more for black equality than a thousand loud speeches cursing Whitey.

This is not the first ruling by Judge Keith of national significance. He is the one who curbed the President's power to eavesdrop on citizens—and the Supreme Court upheld him. It will be a new day in America if the high court upholds him on his job-discrimination decree.

25

I stirred up a lot of brothers and sisters recently with a column in which I said: "Hair ain't where it's at." I was scolding young blacks (and old ones) who go around bulling themselves with the pretense that wearing their hair a certain way proves they have black pride. For a long time it was the Afro, or the "bush," that was supposed to symbolize pride of African heritage. Now they've turned to cornrows, with both men and women sporting this supposedly ancient African hairdo of checkerboard parts and lots of little braids.

The point I want to make is that you can wear your hair any way you please, but it won't guarantee you pride. Only honest achievement can do that. Show me a black college student who makes the honor roll and I'll show you a proud black—even if his head is shaved as clean as a billiard ball. Show me the young black woman who wins top honors in the conservatory of music and I'll show you a proud sister—and it won't matter whether she wears a "fro" or has ironed her locks till they're straight as baling wire.

Black Americans are in a struggle to hang on to what measures of freedom they have gained in that long hard march from slavery. We simply cannot delude ourselves with fads about hair styles, or clothing, to the point that we ignore the reality that we must rely on trained intelligence.

Jews have stood up against centuries of discrimination because they have pursued brainpower with relentless zeal.

Let me emphasize that it *is* progress when black people stop being *ashamed* of being black, or of having kinky hair. It is only when blacks go on to the nonsense of pretending that cornrows or dashikis prove something that the fad becomes self-defeating.

I look at a college student; his massive Afro tells me nothing about him. But let him speak a few sentences and I get a good idea of what is *under* that Afro. I can tell whether he's been spending more time fixing his hair than learning English or physics.

One of the simplest lessons of life is that there is no pride in failure. No kind of hairdo, no so-called African robe, can give genuine self-respect to a young black who goofs off for four years of college and discovers that he or she is unprepared to compete in this society.

So my plea to young blacks is this: think less about hair and more about how to use your brains and skills to guarantee a brighter future for black people—and all of mankind.

26

Black people have been brainwashed in so many ways that millions don't know what to think. They attack the white man and the white government for housing discrimination that leaves blacks herded into ghettos. Yet when a brave black man with the money and the clout forces his way into what has been a lily-white area, do blacks applaud him as a hero? Not all do. Some start dropping poison whispers that "He wants to be white."

I want to do a bit of frank rapping on this black schizophrenia.

For the last few years black people have been deluged by rhetoric about whether integration is a dead dream, or whether "black community control" or black separatism is the wave of the future. Most of this talk is philosophical hogwash. The only thing that should really matter to you and every other black American is: "How do you win by competing in a system that you are not going to change to any great degree?"

Black students note that in four and one-half years in government I held four jobs that 99 per cent of white Americans would have been delighted to have. They want to know if I got those jobs by camping out near the bulletin board so I would learn about juicy job openings before anyone else.

Let me tell you that whether you speak of government or private industry, nobody gets the good jobs by reading civil-service posters or company handouts. The key to success in this society is what I call "the circle of gossip." And that circle operates not at the bulletin board, but on the golf course, at the private club, on the tennis court or at dinner parties.

Big shot Jim Smith has a new government contract coming up, and he needs a new vice-president to oversee it. So while sipping a martini at the club he mentions this to his cronies. Other martini sippers start mentioning people they think are just right for the new job.

Now, if some of Jim Smith's drinking buddies are black, some black people will get recommended for that vice-presidency. If Smith's club is lily-white, the odds are that no black guy's name will ever be mentioned. That good job almost automatically will go to a white man.

My theory is that blacks have got to burrow in, infiltrate, do whatever is necessary to become part of the circle of gossip. Should you join the white professional group, or the Rotary Club, or the country club? You bet your sweet future you should.

It is the white man against whom you must compete eventually, so you had better hear what he hears, read what he reads, know whom he knows. Only that way will blacks ever gain meaningful economic power and rise above this terrible present situation where the normal black family must live on $6,864 a year while the white family has $11,549.

27

Black identity. Black pride. That's what thousands of black students say they are looking for on hundreds of white campuses. But the search has led them onto some strange and sometimes tragic detours of self-segregation. And self-destruction.

Sylvester Monroe is a senior at Harvard. He has written an article for the *Saturday Review of Education* that should be read by every black in college or hoping to go to college.

Blacks at Harvard are like blacks at most colleges. They curse Whitey. They profess to have lost faith in integration. They have isolated themselves into a black corner of the student union. They demand black dorms, black tables in the cafeteria, black newspapers, separate black cheerleaders. Sylvester Monroe is enlightening, and sometimes moving, as he writes of all the factors that led black students to this separatism. But he writes with searing honesty about what black isolation is doing to blacks.

Monroe says black students use "black solidarity" as an excuse to skip classes or avoid anything else they find uncomfortable. They use black solidarity as a cover "to dupe the white community into believing that behind their united front of blackness they are mature, self-confident, and functioning black individuals who know exactly what they want. But what I see and hear instead are insecure and frightened young black men and women."

Monroe quotes a black professor as saying: "The problem with black students at Harvard is that they are too caught up in ideology. Most people who deal in ideologies believe only 10 per cent of it, at most. But blacks at Harvard want to believe 90 per cent of their own ideological bull- - - -."

Monroe quotes a black Harvard dean as saying that several black students now doing B work would be doing A work if they had not isolated themselves from the intellectual strength of Harvard.

Then Monroe talks about the greatest tragedy of all. He says many blacks who bulled their way through Harvard or Yale or other schools found three or four years later that they were ill prepared to compete in the mainstream of American life. Sylvester Monroe is about to walk from Harvard into what he knows is a "complex, demanding white world." He confesses that he feels "very inadequate about my past three years at Harvard, which were lived in an almost totally isolated black vacuum. To be sure, I am thoroughly confused."

Black students will discover a lot more "black pride" when they admit to the same confusion—and when they abandon this isolation that renders them unable to compete.

Cries of "Black Power" no longer are a fad for Afro-American students. Yet I find blacks often ask how black people can attain more of the powers that are essential to first-class citizenship.

It takes many kinds of power to make a people free. Manpower. Dollar power. Brainpower. Fire power. Political power. The power of ideas. In the context of this society, black people are short on all those kinds of power. And the sad truth is that if you don't have one kind of power, you can't get the other kind.

I mean that if you are short on dollar power, you won't be able to afford the schooling, the college training that makes for brainpower. If you don't have manpower, it is hard to achieve political power. It is a vicious circle. But as I said regarding the media, we spend too much time bemoaning our plight, and not enough time using such power as we have.

A lot of brave people, black and white, have been beaten, shot, killed in the struggle to secure the right to vote for black Americans in the Deep South. But millions of blacks all over the country don't care enough to register and vote. Those blacks ought to be ashamed to talk about "political power."

Editors tell me that when I write a stinging column about racism in America they can expect a deluge of letters from whites—especially those disliking me who would like to see me out of the paper. But very few blacks write to encourage the newspaper for carrying a column that says something blacks have passionately wanted someone to say.

Or take the simple matter of buying a daily newspaper. Millions of young people of all races go to school every day without reading a newspaper, and this is appallingly true for black youth. There is an old saying that you can't write if you don't read. I might add that anyone who is a dummy about public affairs can't expect to fare too well in interviews for an important job.

Stop on any campus and some dedicated young black will ask you: "How are we black people ever going to get our thing together?"

There is no sudden, magic formula. Getting our thing together means that each individual does the little things that matter. He votes. He tries to be informed. He sounds off when it counts. He gives whatever help he can to lift another brother or sister. So come on. Let's get it together!

But one thing we blacks *are* coming to understand is that *learning* is power. He who would be free must first destroy the basic enemy of liberty—ignorance . . .

28

We Americans are very proud of our high level of education. Eight out of ten of our children graduate from high school, and 60 per cent of those go on to college. But before we start busting buttons over how smart we are, we might listen to a few sobering facts.

About 21 million Americans over age sixteen can't read well enough to get along in simple everyday living. They can't read help-wanted ads. They have difficulty obtaining a driver's license, a social security card, welfare assistance or Medicare—just because of poor reading ability.

These dismaying figures about illiteracy were reported by poll taker Louis Harris after a survey of more than 1,700 Americans. Not surprisingly, the study showed that reading troubles run highest among the poor and the black. The percentage of blacks who scored low on the tests was almost three times that of whites. If we look at younger persons, we find additional reading problems.

When the late Commissioner of Education James E. Allen, Jr., announced his Right to Read Campaign in 1969, he noted that 10 million American youngsters had significant reading problems. In large city schools, up to half the children read below expectation. And the National Reading Council tells us that many junior colleges report that 30 to 50 per cent of their entering students require reading help before they can start regular studies.

Blacks bear a heavy part of this burden, too.

Allen urged an all-out national effort to end illiteracy in the United States. President Nixon promised new steps to help communities achieve the Right to Read for every young American. But the much-ballyhooed Right to Read program has barely gotten off the ground. Critics contend that the Administration has played a budgetary sleight of hand with the money it was supposed to spend for reading improvement. Others say that the government is strongly committed to the program. As one indication, they point to the appointment of Mrs. Ruth Holloway as director. She is a black woman who formerly was in charge of California's compensatory education program.

It really doesn't help to argue about who is committed to ending illiteracy. Too much is at stake regarding a problem that goes beyond partisan politics. The critical thing is for poor black adults to realize that being unable to read is a serious handicap—like blindness or deformity of the body. But there are relatively easy cures for this invisible handicap of illiteracy.

Every black who truly seeks pride ought to be screaming for programs to end illiteracy. And those who cannot read ought to be quick to use such programs.

29

Twenty years ago a white Southerner said these words to me: "Nigras will be second-class citizens in America until they place more value on trained intelligence. They will always be outnumbered by whites to the extent that anger and violence will be self-defeating. Only when Nigras do like the Jew and put educating their children above whiskey or sororities will they move toward freedom."

If that analysis is true, black people have more to rejoice about these days than they think. There was a time when black people were criticized, legitimately, for wasting their meager dollars while consigning their children to another generation of ignorance. But there are some remarkable signs that black parents have come of age intellectually.

A recent survey of 54,000 college-bound blacks showed that almost half of them came from families earning less than $6,000 a year. Compare that with another survey showing that only 12 per cent of white freshmen came from families earning so little. Allowing for population differences, for every poor white family that sends its kids to college there are now *four* poor *black* families making the sacrifice. Of the 631,000 black undergraduates, only one out of seven come from a family earning over $12,000 a year. That is a remarkable commitment to learning on the part of black families.

These sacrifices have produced fantastic results. In 1965 blacks constituted only 4.6 per cent of undergraduate enrollment, so not even half the blacks were in college who should have been—if they had enrolled according to the black percentage of the population. By 1971, sacrifice had helped to lift the black percentage to 9 per cent—or respectably close to the black 11 per cent of the population.

This has moved foundations, the government, business, to grant scholarships that have opened up snooty institutions that a generation ago enrolled few blacks, or perhaps none.

This has changed higher education profoundly. Choice colleges now concede that their function is not to be country clubs catering to the "elite." They are trying to meet the needs of all the nation.

The most important thing about the upsurge of black collegians is what it means for the future of black people. Every student who studies and learns breathes life into the truism that ignorance is a friend of tryanny, but a learned man is very hard to enslave.

30

If learning is the key to liberty, just how bright is the outlook for black Americans?

I spoke at the University of Florida recently, and I was asked whether blacks are closing the education gap that has for so long put them at a disadvantage in comparison with whites.

As recently as 1965, only 10 per cent of young blacks aged eighteen to twenty-four were enrolled in college. But by 1971 this figure had jumped to 18 per cent, a remarkable increase. Of great significance is the fact that a lot of *poor* blacks were finding ways to get higher education. In 1971, of every eight blacks in college, one came from a family earning less than $3,000 a year.

You can give credit for that to the late Lyndon B. Johnson, who persuaded Congress to pass a law giving substantial aid for higher education. Credit also a lot of corporations that began to finance scholarships for the needy.

But more important than college enrollment is the question of how many blacks finish high school. Let's face it, baby, a black person just can't quite make it in this society without a high school diploma. But as recently as 1970, one black out of every seven was dropping out of high school. Thank heaven we are cutting down the black dropout rate. It fell to one student out of every nine in 1971, and it is still going down.

The sad truth remains that 11 per cent of blacks fourteen to nineteen years old are high school dropouts, compared with only 7 per cent for whites. If you become a dropout, you're in for trouble. First off, you're not likely to have any bread because you probably won't have a job. If you try to get bread some way other than working for it, you're heading for bigger troubles.

The Census Bureau reports that 34 per cent of white men and 50 per cent of black men wind up jobless if they drop out of high school. So it is pretty obvious that dropping out of high school is for fools.

A critical question these days is whether blacks will continue to close the educational gap. The Nixon Administration is talking about educational revenue sharing, and no one knows what it means. Officials at college after college tell me that poor youngsters simply will not get the financial assistance that they have had. This means that those black kids from poverty-level families can kiss their dreams of college goodbye.

Let us fight and argue and pray—and try to ensure that this country never slams the college door in the face of the poor.

But how much faith in education can be clung to by people whose minds have been raped?

For three centuries, black people have been told by white people that they are intellectually inferior—and generations of blacks have believed it and acted accordingly.

In newly integrated classrooms, white teachers are shackled by long-held beliefs that most black children are incapable of learning at a pace comparable to white children. And the teachers' doubts are quickly translated into insecurity and fear on the part of black pupils.

Then someone comes along with a test prepared for whites and interpreted by whites—and uses it on black pupils to prove their "native" inferiority . . .

31

Don't give up on your child because one intelligence test suggests he's backward and cannot make it—especially if your child has lived entirely in a black world and is taking tests keyed to life in the white world.

The case of Harold Howard of Louisville, Kentucky, offers dramatic evidence that thousands of black youngsters are being put down every week because educators don't know how to read their potential.

Harold Howard was in the Kentucky State Reformatory twelve years ago serving a life sentence for armed robbery. Someone there gave him an IQ test and pronounced him "retarded." But today, Associated Press has told the nation, Howard is a straight-A student in the University of Louisville graduate school—even as he holds down a $9,000-a-year job.

Here is a young black man who started the third grade at age fifteen. He breezed through high school and then four years at Kentucky State, where he got a degree in sociology. Two years ago the governor granted him a pardon. How could a "retarded" person do this, you ask. Well, the truth is that Howard never really had an IQ of 69, the level of a moron, as that reformatory test showed.

The tragedy is that many educators in this country are giving up on black youngsters every day because some test suggests they are incapable of learning. Thousands of these kids who might become scientists, doctors, inventors, writers, will be lost forever in the backwaters of misery and despair because no one thinks they deserve a real chance.

I remember my days in Tennessee at the start of World War II. I had buddies with B-plus and A averages who went into the Navy, where the only things they could be were cooks and mess attendants. Their futures died over those vats of beans and cabbages.

No nation can afford to have many Harold Howards. All societies stagnate when so much potential is lost, ignored, stifled. Neither the black race nor any other can achieve freedom without harnessing the full potential of its youth.

One of America's great priorities is to utilize her greatest asset: her people. That means reaching into the city ghettos, the pockets of rural poverty, and mining for the Harold Howards who might be jewels in the rough. But are we so divided, so bent on fighting each other, that no one can take the time to care?

32

This society just can't seem to shake the notion that nature made black people inferior to whites.

Professor Arthur R. Jensen throws a bombshell into the

academic community with his theory that heredity, not environment, makes blacks 15 IQ points dumber than whites.

Dr. William Shockley has polarized the scientific community with a thesis that blacks lack a certain gene common to Caucasians, and that is why blacks are mentally inferior.

Well, a very simple project out in Milwaukee makes Jensen and Shockley look like dummies.

This recurring scream that the Good Lord made black people inferior has influenced a lot of politicians and educators. Both keep asking whether programs like Head Start are a waste of taxpayers' money. Both keep nursing the idea that black children can't be educated in the classic sense, so the only thing to do is give them vocational training.

A remarkable project in Milwaukee makes this kind of talk look stupid. That project has shown that horribly disadvantaged black children can achieve beyond anyone's expectation—if their environment is changed drastically.

A University of Wisconsin team has taken infants from the worst slums of Milwaukee, all of whose mothers had IQs of less than 70 (meaning the moron level), and given them every imaginable stimulation to learn, speak, achieve. This team has intervened in the home life to the extent of giving the mother home-making, baby-care and occupational training.

After four years the IQs of those ghetto youngsters had jumped more than 50 per cent, with some scoring 135. These children, who supposedly could not be educated, were averaging 33 IQ points higher than a control group from their neighborhood that did not get special stimulation. And—mark this: these project children were achieving at a higher level than their age group in the nation as a whole.

Dr. Rick Heber, the University of Wisconsin professor

who heads the program, says his project may prove that it is possible to prevent the kind of mental retardation which occurs in children reared by parents who are both poor and of limited ability.

This Milwaukee project has shown that a mother of low IQ creates an especially crippling environment for her children—above and beyond the ordinary handicaps of the slums.

The cost of that Milwaukee project has averaged about $10,000 per child. Obviously, then, the techniques used to lift the IQs of those children are too expensive to apply on a mass, public-education basis.

What is also obvious is that the problem is not inside black children. It is in a society that leaves them as hopeless victims of the shameful environment so many are born into.

It is easy, of course, to blame "society" for our worst ills. It is especially tempting to do so when our government not only is unhelpful but hostile.

But let us ask rather often what we can do for ourselves and each other . . .

33

I gave a luncheon speech in Chicago recently at which $22,000 was raised immediately for the United Negro College Fund, with the prospect of many thousands more to come. I gave a speech in Washington a couple of weeks ago at which $20,000 was raised for the Legal Defense Fund of the NAACP, with contributions expected to go beyond $50,000.

The amount of money taken in is not what surprised me; it was the large number of blacks involved in the giving and the soliciting. Could it be that fortunate, affluent blacks have now begun to sacrifice to lift those brothers and sisters who need a helping hand?

For a lot of years, blacks who had a *little* money spent an awful lot of it trying to act like whites who had a *lot* of money. Women's clubs blew small fortunes presenting debutantes to society, when the real black society couldn't have cared less. Fraternity groups told stale jokes as they sipped the most expensive whiskeys and dined on the most succulent foods. You were a nobody in Washington, D.C., if you didn't get invited to the formal dances of certain old "girls" clubs where the cost of the perfume alone would have financed a major Supreme Court case.

A lot of that still goes on, as it must, and probably should. Black young women need to feel that they have social pride, too. Anyone who loves to frug or do the boogaloo knows that man and woman do not live by lawsuits alone.

But evidence is all around us that educated, affluent blacks have put the social folderol in a more balanced perspective. They have gotten their thing together, and they are giving money, time, brainpower to the critical business of black liberation.

In many cities around the country you'll find the Girl Friends raising money for scholarships, or the NAACP, or a health program in the Mississippi Delta. You'll find the Links raising money to fight sickle cell anemia, or support those United Negro College Fund institutions that are the only hope of college education for hundreds of thousands of young blacks. Black sororities and fraternities have adopted the truism that the price of black liberation is black sacrifice.

It would be grossly misleading to say that black self-help is everything it ought to be in this country. There is still too much selfishness, too little of the kind of financial commitment to freedom that has enabled Jews to survive centuries of oppression.

But blacks do seem to have concluded that neither white liberals nor the federal government is going to hand them health, wealth, liberty and love on a golden platter. Recognition of that is a vital new step toward freedom.

Whatever else education does, it enhances pride and self-respect.

One of the unfortunate attitudes by black people is their acceptance of propaganda that they inherently tend to become welfare bums . . .

34

Of all the issues in this election campaign, "the welfare mess" may be the most emotional. It is the issue about which Americans have swallowed the most myths and misinformation. The notion abounds that welfare rolls are loaded with able-bodied deadbeats. Stories keep popping up that black women deliberately have illegitimate babies so they can collect more welfare.

In terms of cost, the welfare problem is getting worse. The Department of Health, Education and Welfare reports that in May 1972, just over 15 million Americans received close to $1.6 billion in welfare payments. That's an annual rate of $19 billion.

But look at who gets that welfare money. First, the sick —more than $683 million, or 42 per cent of the May welfare payments, went for medical assistance to the poor, through Medicaid. Another $283 million went to the aged, the blind, the disabled. Still, a whopping $563 million went to help families with dependent children. This is the category that arouses prejudice and anger. A lot of the so-called silent white majority thinks of welfare only in terms of a fat, black, unmarried woman with ten children living in the Waldorf Astoria.

ADC (Aid to Dependent Children) money actually goes to 3 million families with 8 million children—not astounding when you consider that over 5 million families live in poverty in this country. Or that almost 6 million families are headed by women, many of whom have small children and can't work.

But are these needy families sopping up luxury in plush hotels? Hah! The average ADC payment nationally is only $51.40 per person per month. In some of the states where the talk is loudest about black women having babies to get welfare, the payments are absurd: $14.72 per month in Mississippi, $15.41 in Alabama, $19.90 in South Carolina.

Does anyone believe any woman is dumb enough to have a baby, illigitimate or otherwise, just to get $14.72 a month?

It would be nice if we could say that our welfare programs represent the wisdom of a humanitarian society. How wonderful if we could say that welfare programs reflect our belief that every dollar spent on some needy child is bread cast upon the waters, bringing up a harvest of pearls in another generation.

But as I shall show later, welfare is really the darling of businessmen whose cash registers sing a merry tune on the day those welfare checks arrive.

35

There has been a mean campaign to heap shame upon Americans who are on welfare. I call it a mean campaign because it inspires fortunate Americans to hate the unfortunate. It is designed to blind the average American to the truth that American business, not poor people, is the real benefactor of our welfare system.

As I reported earlier, some 15 million Americans receive some kind of welfare payment; the total welfare tab may reach $19 billion this year. But does this mean that the poor are riding a gravy train, dragging overtaxed businessmen to the poor house? Not hardly. The welfare program is a beautiful bonanza for businessmen.

That $19 billion dollars won't stay in the hands of welfare recipients long enough for them to recognize the picture of George Washington. During the worst period of the Nixon recession, welfare money was a lifesaver for thousands of businessmen operating in and around neighborhoods of the poor. In 1970 and 1971, those abused poor people spent $30 billion of welfare money for bread, butter, milk, meat, socks and sheets.

Donald M. Kendall, who is Mr. Pepsi-Cola and a close friend of President Nixon, spoke the unspeakable in 1970 when he told the Whittier, California, Chamber of Commerce that the welfare program is a delightful prop for American business. Kendall was arguing for a welfare program that would double the number of recipients as well as the amount of money going to them. He said to those businessmen: "If we wanted a better prop under our economy we couldn't find one."

Kendall knows that when the government gives $200,000 in cotton price supports to Senator James Eastland of Mississippi, that money may help almost no one but Eastland. He can bury it in the backyard or stuff it in his mattress. But every dollar handed to the poor is spent so fast it is like a direct deposit in some businessman's bank account.

Maybe Mr. Kendall can't think of a better prop for business than the welfare program, but I can.

The government can spend money to provide training for people who cannot earn a living because they were denied an education in the past; because they were being brutalized when the era of advanced technology passed by.

The government can ensure that the children of welfare families are able through education to break the cycle of ignorance, poverty and more ignorance. Then they will become earners contributing far more to the national economy.

But that is a long-range, lasting solution. I am afraid a lot of businessmen would rather have one welfare dollar today than the promise of ten earned dollars tomorrow. So a lot of businessmen will go on assailing welfare recipients, and literally cursing all the way to the bank.

36

If people tell you you're a bum often enough, long enough, sooner or later you'll start believing you're a bum. And acting like one. That's a grim fact of human affairs that lies at the heart of the brainwashing of black Americans.

I've got some facts today to help along some de-brainwashing and to bolster black pride.

For generations, white people in this country described black people as lazy, shiftless, shuffling, oversexed, happy-go-lucky, overgrown children. Blacks could care for the most prized possessions of white people—their children. They could prepare the item most crucial to whites' well-being—their food. Yet whites persisted in saying, and perhaps believing, that blacks were inherently irresponsible.

You don't hear much talk about "shiftless," "happy-go-lucky" blacks any more. But the propaganda is the same. The endless furore about blacks on welfare is just calling black people lazy, irresponsible moochers.

Well, don't let this talk destroy *your* pride. Dr. Andrew F. Brimmer, the noted black member of the Board of Governors of the Federal Reserve System, cites Census Bureau figures as proof that blacks get the bulk of their money the same way whites do: they work for it.

Writing in *Ebony* magazine, Brimmer also notes that 5.2 per cent of the total income of black people comes from public-assistance and welfare payments, whereas only 0.7 per cent of white income is from these sources.

How can one explain this?

Well, whites get 87 per cent of their money from working and the rest from stocks, bonds, rentals of property, interest on savings, etc. Blacks haven't yet earned enough to have stocks, bonds, large savings.

Blacks are predominantly poor. Because of discrimination and deprivation they earned $42.2 billion in 1970, whereas in a truly just society they should have earned $31 billion more.

Brimmer points out that welfare goes to the *poor*, not the *rich*, and if you keep more blacks in poverty, you keep more blacks on welfare.

Maybe the average white American will never accept the truth about welfare. But black people must know the truth. Blacks on welfare are symbols of bigotry and injustice in America. And that is the white man's shame, not the black man's.

Or, the antiblack propagandists suggest that something in the genes pushes blacks toward criminal behavior.

We must not let these slurs blind us to the reality that crime is a curse on, and a challenge to, black communities . . .

37

An elderly woman is mugged on the South Side of Chicago by two teen-age boys. A cabdriver says he had to move from his southeast Washington neighborhood because he was afraid to come home late at night. A young man in Harlem is robbed and murdered on his way home by another young man.

Crime, and the fear of crime, stalk America today. Every segment of society is touched. But nowhere does violence hit harder than in our urban ghettos. And no one is more affected than blacks. For that reason I'll devote my next three commentaries to a discussion of crime and its impact on blacks.

We're all aware—too well aware—that violent crimes have been increasing in the United States. Murder, rape, robbery, beatings. Most of us know a friend or neighbor who's been a victim—if indeed we haven't been victims ourselves.

Surveys show that one person in three living in big center-city areas has been mugged, robbed or burgled, or has had his property vandalized, in the last year. Four persons in ten say they are afraid to walk alone at night in their own neighborhoods.

Violence occurs everywhere, affects everyone. But it has a definite racial overtone. The majority of violent crimes are committed by blacks. The majority of *victims* are black. For example, about 62 per cent of those arrested for murder last year were black. About 55 per cent of the victims were black.

A study by the Metropolitan Life Insurance Company indicates that the homicide rate for nonwhites in America is almost ten times that of whites. A recent *New York Times* survey found that a black resident of New York City is eight times more likely to be murdered than a white resident. *Jet* magazine reports similar ratios in a dozen other major cities.

That same *Times* survey found that 48 per cent of New York homicides involved blacks killing blacks; only 18 per cent crossed racial lines. It simply is not true that most violent crime is committed by blacks against whites. Rather, it usually involves members of the same race. The vice-mayor of Atlanta (now the mayor), a black, says that in his city a black's chances of being robbed are triple those of a white, and a poor black woman is four times as likely to be raped as is a white woman.

Perhaps it is with such figures in mind that a black woman—toughened by a lifetime of living and politicking in Harlem, told a friend, "After Nixon, the person I fear most in the world is the ghetto black teen-ager."

It is not enough to know that blacks are deeply affected by crime, both as perpetrators and victims. We must try to find out why and what can be done.

38

In my last commentary I noted the huge stake that blacks have in the rising tide of violent crime in America. The majority of persons arrested for these crimes are black; the majority of victims are black. In New York City, for example, we saw that a black is eight times more likely to be murdered than is a white.

Today I'll look at some of the reasons behind these fratricidal crimes.

Why are homicide and other violent crimes so high among blacks? Why do black teen-agers mug elderly black women? Why does one black man kill another?

Many theories have been offered about the causes of crime. One which seems to run through most thinking is that poverty is at the root. This is intensified in the case of blacks and other minorities by discrimination. And today we have yet another factor—drug abuse—which has reached epidemic proportion in our ghettos.

Dr. Alvin Poussaint, well-known black psychiatrist, has examined the issue in his book, *Why Blacks Kill Blacks*. He says that economic and social frustration of a segregated people, along with the pressures of poverty, can lead to violent acts against the first available target.

Dr. Poussaint writes: "Frustrated men may beat their wives and children in order to feel manly. Expectedly, these impulses are exaggerated in men who are hungry and without work. Violent acts and crime often become an outlet for a desperate man struggling against feelings of inferiority."

In the same way, it's easy to imagine the example offered in *Jet* magazine by a Chicago minister who works with delinquents. He cites the case of a young boy who drops out of school because he doesn't think the education he is getting is very useful in his everyday world. The boy finds he can't get a good job, which means he can't earn the money he wants. So he winds up taking out his frustrations on those around him. "These people don't mean a thing to him," says the minister. "They become symbols of survival . . . a 19-year-old boy is more likely to snatch a defenseless woman's purse than he is to go downtown and try to hold up a bank."

If you wonder what drives blacks or other oppressed persons to crime, listen to these words from the President's Commission on Violence:

"To be a young poor male; to be under-educated without means of escape from an oppressive urban environment; to want what society claims is available; to see around oneself illegitimate and often violent methods being used to achieve material gain. All this is to be burdened with an enormous set of influences that pull many toward crime and delinquency."

The best hope in combating black-on-black crime may lie with blacks themselves.

39

Murder, rape, assault. Crimes of violence take a terrible toll in this country, and as we've seen in previous commentaries, that toll is highest among blacks.

Is there hope of cutting down this senseless, fratricidal slaughter? The answer to that question lies with blacks themselves.

It would be wonderful if we could count on society to eradicate the root causes of much of today's crime: poverty, discrimination, unemployment. Or if the standard symbols of authority—such as police and government—were respected enough in ghettos so that they could deal with disorder. But such solutions may be a long time coming. And so, more and more, it looks as if it is up to blacks themselves to stop the violence that threatens our society.

Dr. Alvin Poussaint says in his book: "Our black communities can no longer condone blacks hurting blacks. We should have no room for black heroin pushers or black gangsters who prey on the poor. We know that most black people want law and order. We don't want the white society's racist and corrupt law and order, but one that springs from a spirit of brotherhood, justice and judgment by our peers— a system that seeks to rehabilitate offenders, not just to punish them."

Poussaint calls for more community control of the entire judicial system. He urges black policemen, firemen, lawyers and judges to help black communities establish a new type of law-and-order that can control crime and violence.

We should stop making heroes out of black criminals. True, many may be unjustly imprisoned, but that's no reason to hold them up as models our young people should look up to. We must crack down on pushers and deal with addicts— not glorify and glamorize them.

Why is it so vital for blacks to fight crime? In an article in *New York* magazine, black author and teacher Orde Coombs tells us: "We must end crime not because the statistics reveal that we proportionately get arrested for more crimes than whites . . . but because our growth as a black nation and our survival in this country depend on our extirpation of this cancer.

"We cannot talk of advancement in this country unless we lessen crime in our communities, for the specter of disorder inhibits our trust in each other, reduces our stirrings of community, breaks down our fledgling thrusts toward unity, and robs us of the gains of the '60s."

40

It's late in the evening. A woman gets off the bus and starts walking toward her home in one of the city's poverty neighborhoods. A car pulls up alongside and a man asks for directions. Suddenly he leaps from the auto, grabs the woman, drags her into an alley and rapes her.

The circumstances may vary. The attacks may happen in an apartment building or even your own home. They may happen to a young girl who was hitchhiking. But the stark fact is that they are happening—with increasing and frightening regularity. And blacks have a special stake in this unique crime.

Except for a brief period after World War II, the rate of rape cases has gone up steadily in the United States ever since 1930. Today it's the fastest growing crime of violence. Last year there was an average of one rape every ten to fifteen minutes. And that includes only reported cases. For each incident police learn about, there may be three or five or even ten more which are never reported.

For blacks, the crime of rape long has held special significance. Memories of the lynching days still burn in the minds of black men. Between 1872 and 1951, some 1,200 men accused of rape were lynched. Nearly all were Negroes. Out of 455 men executed for rape between 1930 and 1968, 405—or 89 per cent—were blacks.

It is true that a large number of those arrested for rape today are black men—the figure was about 40 per cent in 1970. But a large number of the victims are black women. Studies of police records show that 90 per cent of rape cases involve men and women of the same race.

Often, however, the stories that make the headlines are the few interracial cases, especially those involving a black man and white woman. Black militant leader Eldridge Cleaver, an admitted rapist, gives us some insights into this in his autobiography, *Soul on Ice.*

Cleaver writes: "Somehow I arrived at the conclusion that, as a matter of principle, it was of paramount importance for me to have an antagonistic ruthless attitude toward white women. Rape was an insurrectionary act. It delighted me that I was defying the white man's law and defiling his women. I felt I was getting revenge."

But later Cleaver admitted he was wrong. "I could not approve the act of rape," he wrote. "I lost my self-respect."

What kind of man rapes a woman? Who are the victims and where does the crime occur? Can a woman protect herself?

41

There's no easy way to recognize a rapist. He may be an angry young man who assaults a woman during some petty theft. He may be a mentally deranged sadist, or a mild-mannered family man, or just an ardent chap who gets carried away while necking in the back seat of the car.

Most rapists are young. In one sampling that was studied, 21 per cent were seventeen or younger and only 31 per cent were over twenty-five.

Their motives vary. One major cause, especially in poverty areas, is the mentality of violence so common to the inner city—a violence born of urban pressure and now accepted almost as a part of everyday life. In other cases the cause may be psychological. This rapist—the sick, cruel, sadistic type—is generally considered the most dangerous.

Victims, like attackers, vary greatly. By no means are

they all young and alluring. Every day we read of sexual attacks on tiny children, on pregnant women, on women in their sixties, seventies and eighties.

The assaults occur everywhere—in the laundry room of an apartment building, in college dorms, school yards, alleyways. Some rapists cruise around in cars looking for likely victims. Most of the attacks occur at night and on weekends, though they can take place at any time of day.

What can be done to combat rape? For a start, more police patrols and brighter lights in critical areas. More sensitive handling of the cases, so that women will be more inclined to report them.

Women themselves must play a key role in preventing the attacks and defending against them. Here are a few tips from police:

- Don't walk alone on dark streets.
- Lock your car doors.
- Be suspicious of unknown repairmen or salesmen who come knocking on your door. Give the impression before answering that there's a man in the apartment.
- If you live alone, don't publicize the fact. List your initial instead of first name—M. Adams instead of Mary Adams—so a would-be attacker won't know there is a woman living alone.

Some women are learning karate and other means of self-defense, but police warn that fighting back may make the attacker even more violent.

The crime of rape stems mainly from sickness in our society and the sickness of mentally ill misfits. These are difficult causes to erase, but we must try.

42

Things being what they are, I suppose that integration of any sort ought to be welcomed. The more blacks who work their way into previously all-white endeavors, the better off blacks and the country ought to be. But the *New York Times* has reported a new area—once lily-white—into which blacks are now moving. And I must confess that I'm more inclined to be dismayed than overjoyed. It seems that black racketeers have started to get a piece of the action in organized crime around the country.

When someone talks about black crime, he's usually referring to street crimes: mugging, robbery and small-time drug peddling. Not organized crime. That's been the turf of Whitey, especially the Mafia. But now law enforcement officials say there's evidence that blacks are moving into organized crime in New Jersey, a state where the Mafia has long been entrenched. And black gangs also are reported to be making inroads in Philadelphia, Chicago, New York and other cities with large black populations.

According to these reports, blacks have nudged the Mafiosi out of the slums and entered into working relationships with white racketeers in other black neighborhoods. Under these setups, blacks pay 10 per cent of their gross to whites, and in return get political and police protection.

Blacks also have become loan sharks and bookmakers—a couple of vocations which traditionally were open only to whites. And blacks are moving increasingly into narcotics wholesaling. All of this has led one federal investigator to comment that "Organized crime is probably more integrated than a great majority of law enforcement agencies in New Jersey."

Mind you, it's not that white mobsters are committed to civil rights or are trying to make points with the Equal Employment Opportunity Commission. Rather, the arrangements are based strictly on practical reasons and violence. It's tempting to kid about this, to make cute comments. But, in fact, it is deadly serious and distressing.

These black racketeers are operating almost entirely in black neighborhoods. Their victims are other blacks. That's why whites have not kicked up much of a fuss. If those black hoods start shaking down Whitey, all hell would break lose.

You remember what happened with drug peddlers. When the drug problem was limited to the ghetto, no one worried very much. But as soon as it spread to the suburbs and other middle-class areas, then the whole nation got worked up.

Well, if white society is not concerned about black racketeers, then blacks darn well ought to be. I can only repeat what I said in a previous commentary. There's no excuse for glorifying a crook or racketeer just because he's black. A black mobster is no more credit to *his* race than a Mafioso is to the Italians.

Surely no aspect of criminality in America has had a more corrosive effect on black communities than the drug traffic.

But don't forget that alcohol is a drug!

43

It's after midnight. In a darkened slum hallway a young boy straps a rubber tube around his arm and plunges a hypodermic needle into his vein. Heroin has another victim. From apartment halls to school halls, from Harlem to Beverly Hills, the problem of drug abuse pervades American society. And nowhere is it more cruel and destructive than in black communities. Today we'll take the first of several probing looks at this scourge.

The headline in the newspaper read simply: "DRUG USE INCREASES IN SCHOOLS HERE." That particular story referred to Washington, D.C. But the same headline could appear in practically any newspaper, for drug misuse knows no boundaries.

Millions of Americans—a great number of them black —flirt with danger through the inappropriate use of drugs of all kinds. Trafficking in drugs has become one of the biggest enterprises in the United States—and one of the most profitable.

Last year a billion and a half dollars' worth of illicit drugs and narcotics was seized, including two tons of heroin. But at the same time addicts spent more than a billion dollars on heroin alone. What do they get for their money?

They get malnutrition and disease—hepatitis, malaria, tetanus. They get ruined lives. As the habit grows, addicts become incapable of holding a job and start stealing or selling personal belongings to get money to buy more drugs. Women turn to prostitution. More than 100,000 persons lead totally unproductive lives because of drugs, according to the Bureau of Narcotics and Dangerous Drugs. It is estimated that one third to one half of all the holdups, burglaries, muggings and thefts in our cities are committed by heroin addicts.

And some get death. In New York City the greatest single cause of death among adolescents and people aged fifteen to thirty-five is narcotics addiction. The death toll from drugs in New York City is greater than the death toll in the Vietnam war for all of New York State.

The drug plague can strike anywhere. No child is immune, no home, no school, no neighborhood. This cancer that sprouted in ghettos and slums has spread to middle-class suburbs, high schools and colleges, the armed services, and industry.

Nowhere is the cost of drug abuse—in human and social and physical terms—higher than in the ghettos. And nothing in the drug scene is more dismaying than the growing use of heroin among young blacks.

44

I pointed out in my last commentary how great a curse drugs have become, especially to the minority groups in the great cities of America. Today we'll take a look at the lost lives, the lost property, the dead dreams—because too many young blacks are *suckers* for the fads created by evil, greedy drug peddlers.

The ordinary black youngster faces a variety of temptations in the drug field. He or she is told that to be "one of the gang" it is a must to try marijuana, better known as pot, weed, grass. Many kids give in.

One of the current fads is barbiturates, commonly known as sleeping pills. They cause slurring of speech, staggering, quick tempers that often lead to fatal fights. Then there are the hallucinogens, the most famous being LSD, which produce hallucinations, illusions and sometimes crippling or fatal mental defects. And of course there are the narcotics— mainly heroin—which are the leading killers among drugs.

In virtually every black community in America there is someone trying to peddle one or all of these drugs to black children. It's hard to get precise figures on drug abuse among blacks. But we have some disturbing approximations. The Bureau of Narcotics and Dangerous Drugs found that 50 per cent of the active addicts that it recorded were black. One conservative estimate puts the number of black addicts at 270,000.

Jet magazine reports that 3,100 blacks died last year from heroin alone. And that doesn't include those who committed suicide or were killed in the commission of drug-related crimes.

Why such widespread drug abuse among blacks? Like Hollywood stars, sports heroes, suburban youth, there is the hunger for new excitement. There is depression, or loneliness, hopelessness, foolish curiosity. But for black youngsters there is the added pressure of pride-crushing bigotry, discrimination—the mental emasculation of black people.

And there is the simple truth that the kingpins of the underworld decided long ago to make black people the special victims of the drug traffic. Remember the book and movie *The Godfather*? The Mafia Don says cruelly that black people have no pride, so "let them lose their souls with drugs."

I say black youngsters do have pride. But I hope that at least they have brains enough to accept what the late great Billie Holiday said in her autobiography: "All dope can do for you is kill you. And kill you the long, slow, hard way. And it can kill the people you love right along with you."

45

We think of the drug problem as a semiliterate derelict, stealing a ring or radio to pay for his habit. Or a poorly educated woman debased to the point of selling her body. Or of tragic babies, born addicted to heroin or methadone from their mothers' wombs. But the drug problem is also a scourge of the campus, posing a grave threat to a new generation of black leadership.

Dr. Charles S. Ireland is administrator of Freedmen's Hospital at predominantly black Howard University. The traffic at that hospital gives Dr. Ireland a perceptive view of the extent of the drug problem. He said to me: "If the drug-abuse problem among the young escalates for another five years as it has in the past five years, the drain on the pool of potential leaders in this country will be seriously affected for at least one generation. When inequities of educational advantage for black students is taken into consideration, the loss of a single potential black leader is out of all proportion to that in other groups."

I asked Dr. Ireland about some of the drug tragedies

that he has seen. He replied: "Perhaps the most pitiful incident that I have seen occurred during the hospitalization of a heroin pusher following a gunshot wound. Before the nurses and attendants on the ward understood what was going on, streams of people of all ages and descriptions were desperately defying the rules of the hospital to make contact with their pusher, their supplier of heroin. The mildest-looking men, women and youngsters were animal-like in their defiance of any effort to keep them away from him. Naturally, this was stopped, but the complete dependence of these people on this man was a devastating facet of the human condition."

Dr. Ireland warns that the use of all kinds of drugs, legal and illegal, has been foisted upon the weak and stupid to make money. He pleads with students to realize that there are no safe drugs for depression, sleeplessness, inattentiveness, boredom or anxiety.

He pleads with those who have a drug problem to seek care at his hospital with an assurance that they will be regarded as sick people, not criminals. He begs students not to try sophomoric remedies on their pals in the case of a drug overdose. That, he says, is a formula for unnecessary deaths.

Fights with boyfriends and girl friends, tough examinations, the desire to be popular can make college a difficult, depressing time. But drugs offer no cheap route to happiness. I asked Dr. Ireland to sum up his message to college students. He said: "There is a need for them to understand that no one feels good all the time, and that the price for feeling good all the time through the use of drugs is addiction, enslavement and destruction."

46

Are there ways to fight the scourge of drugs? Can the supply of heroin be cut off? Can addicts be rescued? What can you and I do to save our children and our neighborhoods?

The battle against drug abuse is being fought on several fronts. The most publicized is the effort to halt the smuggling of heroin and marijuana. But for each French Connection that is disconnected, scores of illegal shipments sneak through.

So we have set up a variety of programs to help those who are hooked. One approach is rehabilitation. You find places like Synanon, where addicts are treated in a non-medical group-living atmosphere. Another method gaining in usage involves the substitution of methadone for heroin. Methadone is not as addictive, and it allows the patient to function more normally. Great Britain has gone a step further. It operates a plan under which certified addicts get free doses of heroin. This doesn't cure anyone, but it keeps them from committing crimes to get heroin money.

There is no easy solution to the drug-abuse problem. Perhaps that is why many persons want to take matters into their own hands. Many law-abiding blacks talk of forming vigilante groups to deal with pushers. They agree with Julian Bond when he says: "Let the sellers of poison to our children know that the price of drugs is death at the hands of the community." That's tough talk, but it can lead to jail terms for murder.

What else is possible?

Form drug-abuse education committees within social and fraternal groups or community organizations. Set up exhibits, provide information and displays to schools. Work with law-enforcement officials and with newspapers, radio and television.

As parents, set good examples for your children. Talk frankly with them, and *listen* to them. Teach that the stresses of life can be solved without drugs. Know the signs of drug abuse—things like a change in school attendance or grades, wearing sunglasses at odd hours to hide dilated pupils or long-sleeved shirts to hide needle marks.

If you suspect that drug tragedy has struck your home, family or neighborhood, don't be afraid to act. Sometimes you'll need help. The Heroin Hotline has been set up to take information on drug trafficking. Call 800-368-5363. There's no charge, and you won't have to give your name.

The battle against drug abuse is not simply the responsibility of police or teachers or government. Drugs are everyone's problem. And you had better believe it.

47

If you were asked, "What's the number-one drug problem in the United States?," what would your answer be?

Marijuana? Heroin? LSD? Barbiturates?

Surprisingly, it is none of those.

It's alcohol, by a wide margin, says the National Commission on Marijuana and Drug Abuse. In a recent report, the commission stated that alcohol users far outnumber the users of all other drugs, and that vulnerable groups are especially dependent on it.

It's understandable if you did not guess the right answer. A lot of people don't consider alcohol a drug. But it definitely is, says the commission. A powerful and habit-forming one. And a dangerous one. Medical authorities say that alcoholism ranks with heart disease and cancer as one of our leading health problems.

The use of alcohol is widespread. Retail sales of wine, beer and hard liquor amounted to over $24 billion in 1971. Or, looking at it another way, Americans drank almost 4½ billion gallons of those beverages that year.

Some 95 million Americans drink. And 9 million of them are considered alcoholics. I'm not talking about the stereotyped drunks staggering on skid row. Most alcoholics are like the rest of us—men and women of all ages, races, colors. They're married, have good homes and families.

According to one recent study, men from upper socioeconomic classes have their worst drinking problems when they're in their twenties and thirties, and they appear to grow out of them as they reach their forties and fifties. Lower socioeconomic groups, on the other hand, show an increase in drinking problems in the forty-five to forty-nine age bracket.

Whatever class they come from, alcohol abusers cost a lot of money and grief. An estimated $15 million a year is lost in property damage, work time, health and welfare costs due to alcoholism. About half of the traffic deaths involve drinking, and one third of the murder victims have high alcohol content in their blood. Over half of the suicide victims in this country have been found to be chronic alcoholics.

And the divorce rate among alcoholics is four times the national average.

Drinking isn't all bad, you may answer. Doesn't alcohol increase sexual aggressiveness and relax sexual anxieties? Don't count on it. Scientific opinion is sharply divided on that point.

Here in America we've usually treated alcohol problems in the courts and through law and punishment. That approach is now considered doubtful. Authorities say that alcoholism can be successfully dealt with, mostly by counseling, therapy and other medical and psychological methods.

In future commentaries I'll look more closely at getting help for alcoholics, and at two special groups of drinkers—young people and women.

48

America's young people have found a potent, sometimes addictive, and legal drug. It's called alcohol.

Drinking is nothing new for teen-agers. In fact, it's a kind of ritual of youth. In recent years, however, a great many youngsters from all walks of life have turned to drugs like marijuana, heroin and barbiturates. Reports coming in now from schools and national studies tell us that there's a change occurring. The newest way for kids to turn on is an old way—with alcohol.

Listen to these words of a high school senior in Brooklyn, as told to a reporter from *Newsweek* magazine: "A lot of us used to smoke pot, but we gave that up a year or two ago. Now my friends and I drink a lot . . . and in my book, a high is a high."

Why are youngsters rediscovering booze? One reason is pressure from other kids to be one of the gang. Another is the ever-present urge to act grown-up. For some, it eases the burden of problems at home or at school. And it's cheaper. You can buy a couple of six-packs of beer for the price of three joints of pot.

Perhaps the main reason is that parents don't seem to mind. They tolerate drinking—sometimes almost seem to encourage it. In part this may be due to the fact that parents themselves drink; in part it's because they're relieved to find that their children are "*only*" drinking, and are not involved with pot, LSD or other drugs.

What these parents may not realize is that alcohol is also a drug, and a potentially dangerous one. Furthermore, few are aware just how young the drinkers are these days. The National Council on Alcoholism reports that in 1972 the age of the youngest alcoholics brought to its attention dropped from fourteen to twelve. Other studies have found that three fourths of senior-high students have used alcohol —an increase of 90 per cent in three years. And 56 per cent of junior-high students have tried alcohol.

The Medical Council on Alcoholism warns: The potential teen-age drinking problem should give far more cause for alarm than drug addiction. Many schools have reacted to teen-age drinking. They've started alcohol-education programs. But a lot of experts feel that teen-agers are not going to stop drinking until adults do.

Next time I'll talk more about adult alcoholics, especially women, and how to help them.

49

Of the 9 million or so alcoholics in America, it's estimated that nearly one-third are women. And that figure may be low, because a great many women hide their drinking problems. The majority are quiet, stay-at-home drinkers, and sometimes it takes years to detect their alcoholism.

We hear a lot about the suburban housewife and her drinking problems. But, in fact, alcoholism among women is not limited to the suburbs. You find it in the inner city as well, in small towns and large. The underlying reasons which lead women to drink are universal: boredom, depression, problems with marriage, loneliness, children leaving home.

One new study indicates that alcoholic women drink to feel more womanly. It found that married alcoholic women more often had some kind of obstetrical or gynecological trouble than their nonalcoholic counterparts—maybe trouble conceiving a child, or frequent miscarriages. These women saw something wrong with themselves as women and as a result turned to drinking. It offered a temporary sense of freedom, well-being, warmth.

Unfortunately, heavy drinking works in the opposite way. Eventually, the woman feels less of a woman. She neglects her appearance, can't cope with her home and family, is shunned by friends.

Can anything be done to help these women? And the millions of male alcoholics? And the young people we've seen turning from drugs to alcohol?

Strictly speaking, there is no "cure" for the alcoholism. It is a form of drug addiction and as such involves physical and psychological dependence. But it can be slowed down and treated—if the alcoholic seeks help.

The best-known program is Alcoholics Anonymous, a worldwide organization of former alcoholics who help one another kick the habit. AA charges no fees. The only requirement for membership is a desire to stop drinking. Chapters are listed in local phone books.

Churches, civic groups, social agencies and the government also have programs which deal with the problems of alcoholism, and can provide information and advice. The National Council on Alcoholism, a voluntary health organization, will furnish educational information. You can write to the Council at 2 Park Avenue, New York 10016.

Remember, the alcoholic is not a doomed person. He or she can recover—if he'll seek help and stop drinking.

Part IV

Black Perspectives on Black Families

The terrible tragedy for most of us black Americans is that we have not recovered from those days of slavery when the "master" viewed family life as something too good, too civilized, or too costly to him, for black people to enjoy.

Trauma, conflict, dislocation, lack of tradition —these are still overriding factors in too many black families.

Some of us are breaking through the psychological, emotional and even physical prisons that the slave masters built around us.

But we are not yet honest enough with ourselves or each other. We have got to stop worrying that Whitey will learn the truth about our weaknesses, our faults. Since the white man controls all the media, he has the power to declare his own truths.

We must stop being overly sensitive and defensive—evidence is everywhere that no race has a monopoly on crime, violence, corruption, drug addiction, alcoholism, greed . . . or promiscuity.

But we dare not blind ourselves to the ways

in which these things strike harder and deeper into the black community. Nor can we cease to probe the reasons why . . .

50

Let someone mention the illegitimacy rate, or the welfare problem, and you know the stereotype notions that lurk in the background. Black men are thought of as oversexed animals, black women as sluts bearing children to get charity. A sociology professor at Howard University has interviewed more than nine hundred women in several states and come up with evidence that blacks are among the most prudish people in America.

Dr. Robert E. Staples, who earned his doctorate at the University of Minnesota, cites his five-year study as evidence that a person's class level is what determines sexual attitudes and mores. Because there is little privacy in lower-class homes, he says, lower-class children are exposed early to overt sexual activity. They imitate adult sexual activity. This will explain why so many poor girls (and that means many minority-group girls) have illegitimate babies.

But Staples says blacks have been imitating the Puritan ethic that for so long dominated sexual values in the white culture. Spurred on by the abuses and degradation of slavery, middle-class black women have become more Puritan than the Puritans. Thus, while mores in the white community become more lax in the current sexual revolution, black middle-class women cling to their new Puritanism so strongly that Staples finds them to be less promiscuous. He says black women "have fewer partners and engage in fewer acts than white women today."

Dr. Staples says there are some strong pressures on black women to be more permissive sexually. First, he notes, there are about a million more black women in the country than men. The statistical disparity is even greater, he says, when a college-educated black female hopes to attract a college-educated black male. So when ebony-skinned Joe College tells the girl she must come across, she is under a lot of emotional pressure.

Studies of things as emotional and complicated as sexual mores and attitudes can never be a precise science. Thus a lot of sociologists will disagree with some of Staples's conclusions. Yet anyone of any race who has been poor knows how much overt sex and how much sexual trauma the average child is exposed to. There can be no doubt that a lot of illegitimacy, promiscuity, venereal disease flow directly from poverty, poor housing, lack of privacy. It may well be that rape and other sexual crimes flow out of the same social aberrations.

One of these days, perhaps, we will stop cursing unwed mothers and thumbing our noses at welfare recipients long enough to do something about the problems of poverty, pigsty housing, childhood trauma. We just might find the key to a lot of our social woes.

51

The Washington *Post* brought us some good news and some bad news recently insofar as illegitimate babies are concerned.

✴ First the bad news: in 1972, more than half the black babies born in the nation's capital were born out of wedlock.

Now the good news: although the percentage went up, the actual number of illegitimate babies declined from 5,740 to 5,359. The reason the percentage went up is that Washington's married black women had 1,232 fewer babies in 1972 than they did in 1971.

Washington, D.C., is not much different from other big cities in America. An illegitimate birth is a grievous social problem that brings sorrow, shame, angry recriminations into thousands of homes. Beyond that, we know that when white Americans read a glaring headline saying "51 PER CENT OF BLACK BIRTHS ILLEGITIMATE," this stigmatizes the entire black race. It is seized by bigots as proof that blacks are "just animals" and that they do not deserve the opportunities and rights accorded to white Americans.

So, from the standpoint of happiness and stability within the black family, or progress by black people as a whole, we have to be pleased that the number of births out of wedlock is declining. We must learn how to make it decline faster.

That Washington *Post* story reported that the number of illegitimate babies born in the black community is way out of proportion to the number born in the white community. Whites accounted for about 12 per cent of the babies born in the District of Columbia last year, but whites produced only 2.7 per cent of the illegitimate babies.

Babies born out of wedlock are largely a reflection of poverty, social deprivation and simple ignorance—yes, ignorance, especially in this era of the birth-control pill. We've known for years that morality is not racial. White girls with educated, protective parents, or who know how to protect themselves from pregnancy, or who have access to abortions, rarely wind up chained for life to an illegitimate child.

We can strive for higher moral standards in all communities. But we must also push for greater sexual education among blacks, especially young females. We must see that clinics and birth-control pills and devices are readily available to all who want them.

I would wager that for every hundred black babies born out of wedlock, seventy-five grow up into lives of misery. And of the hundred mothers, fully half go on to live far sadder lives than might otherwise have been the case.

Through science and education, we can do something to ease this problem—and we must.

52

You hear a lot of talk these days about a "sexual revolution" taking place among America's young people. Parents are shocked when their son brings home a girl friend and announces they'll be sharing his bedroom. Or they wince when they see pictures of young folks gamboling in the nude at some rock concert.

Well, none of this proves that today's teen-agers really do have rounder heels than did yesterday's. But there is little doubt that they are active sexually, and there's little doubt that a great many are not so wise in these matters as they may think. As a result, a lot of youngsters are in for sorrow and distress if we don't recognize what's happening and deal with it openly.

A recent nationwide survey found that 28 per cent of the unmarried girls fifteen to nineteen years old admitted they had had sexual relations. Among blacks, the figure was 54 per cent—more than one out of two.

In the last year for which there are figures, more than 600,000 children were born to teen-agers. And more than one fourth of these were out of wedlock. The rate of illegitimacy among teens increased two to three times between 1940 and 1968. Teen-agers will bear some 200,000 illegitimate children this year.

I don't cite these figures to shock you or prove there's a sex explosion. Rather, they are intended to show the roots of a serious problem. For a teen-ager, pregnancy carries bleak physical, emotional and social prospects for both mother and child, especially if the girl is not married, and especially if she's black.

Pregnancy is the number-one cause of dropouts among girls in high school. The suicide rate for teen-age mothers is ten times that of the general population. The babies of unwed teens are more likely to be premature and mentally retarded or to die before they're a year old. Those illegitimate children who live grow up in a society that regards them as socially, morally and legally inferiors.

The incredible thing is that so many young people engage in so much sexual activity and know so little about it, and that so many adults cling to the outmoded notion that if they can just keep discussions of sex out of the schools, these awful problems will go away.

An indication of the lack of information was given by a fifteen-year-old New York girl testifying before the Commission on Population Growth. She said many of her classmates—all high school students—didn't have a clear picture of how babies are made. And in their hygiene class, when one student asked the teacher what method of contraception she would recommend for fifteen-year-olds, the teacher answered, "Sleep with your grandmother."

In a report last year, the population commission offered several recommendations for dealing with sex ignorance and with the adolescent mother and her child. In the next edition of "Black Perspectives," I'll discuss these.

53

Last time I talked about the increased sexual activity among teen-agers and the ostrichlike attitude that many parents and other adults have taken toward it. One group that didn't react this way was the Commission on Population Growth and the American Future. It made several recommendations on that subject—controversial ones, as you might expect, but well worth pursuing.

The commission emphasizes that ignorance does not prevent sexual activity, but it does promote undesirable consequences, like venereal disease and unwanted pregnancies. So the population commission recommended that appropriate family planning material be developed and worked into school courses.

Ideally, of course, sex education should be taken care of at home, but in many homes, that's just not possible or likely to happen. So it should be presented in a responsible way through community organizations, the mass media and, especially, the schools.

It isn't enough, though, just to tell adolescents about birth control. They should be able to do something about it, but the laws in many states prevent them from getting contraceptive information and services. The commission recommended that states permit minors to receive such information and services in appropriate, sensitive ways.

That doesn't mean setting up vending machines in school cafeterias. Rather, the approach might be teen-age clinics along the lines of those set up by Planned Parenthood in San Francisco and several other cities. At these clinics, kids come for rap sessions, counseling, discussions of pregnancy and contraception. And they can get birth-control devices.

The best sex ed courses and teen clinics will not prevent all unmarried girls from getting pregnant. Those who do often face a lonely, frustrating and dangerous future. They're expelled from school, shut off by family and friends, vulnerable to medical complications. In short, likely candidates for welfare.

In recent years a number of educational, social and health programs have been started to aid these girls. They offer them a chance to continue their high school studies, receive regular medical care and personal counseling. These programs should be expanded. Finally, we should remove the stigma placed on the 300,000-plus children born out of wedlock each year to mothers of all ages. All children should get fair and equal status, regardless of the circumstances of their birth.

Some of the things I've been talking about are hard for a lot of people to swallow. They may seem to condone or even promote sexual activity. That is *not* their purpose, of course. They aren't meant to condone or condemn. They simply face up to reality. And they can help make life a little more hopeful and healthy for tens of thousands of young mothers and their babies.

54

This country has at least *tried* to face up to a lot of evil prejudices in the last generation. Against black people. And women. And Spanish-speaking Americans. And the foreign-born. Even the aged. But one increasingly large group was for a long time neglected. I refer to the millions of Americans born to unwed parents. Finally the courts and millions of Americans are awakening to the fact that those born out of wedlock are God's children, too.

Almost every American senses the stigma of illegitimacy. Most Americans have counted the months after a marriage often enough to know that there is even a stigma attached to being *conceived* out of wedlock.

But did you know that until five years ago, Louisiana held that an illegitimate child could not recover damages for the wrongful death of his or her mother? Or that insurance companies were getting away with the contention that a child born out of wedlock could not receive his dead father's workmen's compensation payments?

Did you know that Texas law obliged a father to support his legitimate child, but not his illegitimate offspring?

Prejudices and discriminations against illegitimate children are so great, so sinister, that perhaps no other group in America is more likely to turn to crime, or homosexuality, or the psychiatrist, or suicide.

This is of special concern to black Americans because from the first days of slavery, black families were forbidden or broken up. For a tragic variety of reasons, blacks bear a disproportionate number of illegitimate babies in America. It should be noted, though, that Caucasians are more and more responsible for the fact that over 300,000 illegitimate babies a year are now born in this country.

So Americans of all races can rejoice that the "civil rights" movement in the courts finally has embraced the illegitimate child. The U.S. Supreme Court struck down Louisiana's discriminations, and it told insurance companies that illegitimate children are entitled to their dead daddies' workmen's compensation.

Justice William O. Douglas noted that illegitimate people must submit to the draft and fight for this country; they pay taxes like everyone else.

Justice Lewis F. Powell, Jr., said for the Supreme Court: "No child is responsible for his birth, and penalizing an illegitimate child is an ineffectual—as well an unjust—way of deterring the parent."

Yet, deep prejudices and passions remain. Millions of Americans still rejoice at casting the first stone. And not at the adult they adjudge to have sinned, but at the child who is the hopelessly innocent offspring.

The legal changes in the courts are encouraging. But no conscience can be clear until in our hearts we accept a human being as a human being, casting aside old prejudices about accidents of birth.

55

A lot has been written about the plight of black children, and the black family, in America. But not enough has been said about the growing phenomenon of divorce and what it portends for the future of black people.

Divorce has become commonplace in this country for all racial groups. The Census Bureau says that in March 1972 there were 139,000 marriages and 76,000 divorces and annulments. This is worse than one marriage breaking up for every two marriages that take place. And that breakup rate is four times worse than it was for the year 1960.

But it is among blacks that divorce takes a very horrible toll. One Census study showed 37 per cent of all black families headed by a woman. In over half of those cases, divorce or separation was the reason.

Deprivation is close to a certainty for black children where a woman is head of the household. In selected low-income areas, Census found that the normal family headed by a woman has an income of only $3,900 a year. This compares with $7,800 for such families headed by a male.

Studies show that in poverty-level families, only 24 per cent of black children and 44 per cent of white children live with both parents. This means that three fourths of the poor black children in America grow up either without a mother or without a father figure. Most women who head families work, depriving the children of the guidance and security of having Momma in the house.

Small wonder, then, that so many black children are lured into delinquency and crime.

Small surprise that so many black girls have illegitimate babies.

Understandable that the drug peddler finds it so easy to prey upon young blacks.

Perhaps the greatest curse of all is that divorce sets in train a vicious cycle. Youngsters who never knew a stable home are bad bets for marriage. Poor, deprived youngsters tend to become poor, deprived adults.

There is no point in lecturing black couples not to rush to the easy divorce . . . especially when the national trend is to split up at the slightest provocation. Nor is there any point in pretending to offer solutions; the factors that make for a high divorce rate are too complicated for that.

But we know that getting more money into black families would help. So a guaranteed minimum income would help stabilize some families. We know that better guidance and counseling for young blacks must come from schools and churches.

Beyond that, we can keep hammering home the tragic facts about what divorce and separation are doing to blacks as a people.

56

We know that many black families in America are headed by women, not by adult males. It's also true that census takers have had a hard time finding all the nonwhite males. As many as 10 per cent went uncounted in the 1970 census.

One of the assumptions has been that a great many black men and boys were purposely in hiding—perhaps to avoid a welfare case worker. The truth may be that many of those men were dead, for, in fact, the black man is something of a scarce commodity.

Jacquelyne Jackson, an associate professor at Duke University Medical Center, has made a fascinating study of black men. It was reported a while back in *Ebony* magazine.

Dr. Jackson points out that for the last fifty years, the ratio of black males to black females has gone down steadily. In 1920 there were 99 black men for every 100 black women. By 1970 the ratio was 91 to 100. It's not simply that black men are missing when census takers or welfare workers go out to find them. They are just not here, says Dr. Jackson.

Up through the age of fourteen, there are roughly the same number of black males as females. But from fifteen on, the drop in the black male population is startling. For example, there are only 83 black men per 100 women in the thirty-five to forty-four age group, and only 84 per 100 in the twenty-five to thirty-four bracket.

Why such a gap?

One explanation suggested by Dr. Jackson is that black

males generally die earlier than black females from heart and lung diseases, chronic alcoholism, auto and industrial accidents, homicide, suicide and drug addiction. In addition, she notes, the availability of black males is further reduced by those who are in prison, those killed in war and those who marry whites.

The leading cause of premature death among black men may be violence. According to Professor Lee Robin of Washington University Medical School, the homicide rate among Negro men aged twenty-five to forty-four is twelve times the white rate. A black man in that age bracket is more likely to be murdered than a white man is to die in an accident—which is the chief cause of death among young white males.

The most immediate result of the lack of black men clearly is to cut the number of potential husbands for black women. This helps explain why a disproportionate number of black families are headed by women, and it has significant implications for those families.

It is commonly thought that the great number of matriarchal families is due to the fact that many men are unemployed, poorly educated or staying away because of welfare laws. But Dr. Jackson says that this is not true. There just aren't enough black men available.

"Even if all available black males were to make highly significant gains in their education, occupational and income levels tomorrow, some black households would still be headed by women and some black women still would be without mates," says Dr. Jackson. Thus, the black matriarchal family is a product of necessity and reality.

How do we go about dealing with the reality and basic problem—the lack of black men?

For one thing, Dr. Jackson believes, it's time to be more concerned about improving the lives, opportunities, education and income of black women, since they'll probably continue to be heads of households in many cases. It's not true, according to Dr. Jackson, that black women are better educated or get better jobs than black men. On the contrary, they usually have access to the worst jobs at lowest earnings.

Another approach is to increase the supply of black men. Lengthen their lifespan through better access to health care. Reduce the number who are railroaded into jails, juvenile detention homes, and the like.

"It would also help to improve the socioeconomic levels of black males," she says. "Black females who are seriously concerned about themselves and their men and their children can no longer be arrogant enough to assume that they have arrived, and that the only remaining task is to raise their men to their level."

Black women, says Dr. Jackson emphatically, have not yet arrived.

The deep malaise within families reflects itself in many ways—some pathetic, some cruel. Child abuse is one of the cruelest . . .

57

The little girl was carried into the emergency room by her mother. Her face and arms were badly bruised. One eye was swollen shut. The distraught mother told the doctor that the child had fallen down the stairs at their home.

X-rays and a check of medical records revealed that the child had suffered similar injuries before. The doctor became suspicious. He reported the case to a special team, which talked to the girl's mother and father. It was then that the truth came out: the youngster had not fallen downstairs; she had been beaten by her parents.

It seems incredible, but every year children in America are beaten with baseball bats, broomhandles and fists. They are whipped with electric cords and belts. They are burned, scalded, stabbed and bitten. Many are scarred or maimed. Some die.

Nobody is sure just how many battered babies there are. One educated guess is at least sixty thousand a year. In addition, scores of thousands more are neglected, or sexually abused.

For a long time, very little was done about child abuse in the United States. Our laws were more concerned about cruelty to animals than cruelty to children. In the last decade an all-out effort has been launched to discover and remedy the situation. It's being waged in many areas . . . state legislatures, hospitals, courtrooms, welfare agencies, homes.

The key to dealing with child abuse lies in identifying and working with parents and the other adults who abuse children. Battering parents come from all segments of society, but some studies indicate a greater risk among the poor. There's a logical explanation for this if it's true. The poor face additional stresses, like finances and unemployment, which could trigger the outbursts.

What can be done about child abuse?

Probably the most successful program is being carried on at the University of Colorado Hospital in Denver. There pediatricians, psychiatrists, social workers and others have formed a Child Protection Team which is trained to spot cases, then deal with them in a variety of ways. One of the team's innovations is a program in which women work with abusive parents. They offer the love, concern and friendship that these parents have lacked.

Another technique is borrowed from Alcoholics Anonymous—only in this case it's Parents Anonymous. Abusive parents get together to talk out their problems and help one another. Los Angeles, New York and Denver are among the places where such groups are in operation.

There is no sure cure for adults who batter children, no single form of treatment. But ways are opening to deal with these people and to help them so that more and more abused youngsters can return to their own homes and live there safely.

These kinds of problems are solved by people, not time.

Expenditures of funds for vast social programs can help, but everything fails in the absence of wise leadership. Black America has suffered some terrible leadership losses in recent years—among whites as well as blacks.

We are now painfully aware that the quality of leadership makes a crucial difference in a free but complex society . . .

58

The last years have taken a heavy toll of black leadership in America. Death has claimed Martin Luther King, Whitney Young, Ralph Bunche and Jackie Robinson, among others. What does this mean to the future of black people?

It is pointless to ask who will replace men like King, Young, Bunche or Robinson. Men of their peculiar qualities are never really replaced. They were creatures of a time and circumstance that we shall not see again. What we must expect, then, are new black leaders with new styles and tactics suited to the new status and new problems of black people.

The happy truth is that the potential for black leadership is now greater than it has ever been. In 1970, about 470,000 black men and women were in college. That is eight times the number who were in college in 1950 when Ralph Bunche won the Nobel Prize, and Jackie Robinson's name had just become a household word. What it means is that we can now expect black leadership to come from a much broader spectrum of professions.

There was a period when a few college presidents and preachers formed the heart of black leadership. Then came the era of the civil rights organizations, with the Urban League and the NAACP in the forefront. It was taken as automatic that whoever headed those organizations was regarded as a national black leader. These leaders of civil rights groups were consulted by Presidents, invited to the White House, asked to visit foreign countries. They were leaders by virtue of their jobs.

Now, as vast numbers of blacks emerge from colleges and universities we are bound to see new black contributions to science, medicine, journalism, diplomacy, government, commerce, politics. We will still have civil rights groups whose leaders are routinely considered national leaders. But many more blacks will be regarded as leaders by virtue solely of their scholarship, their achievements, their impact on their fields of endeavor. This will make it much more difficult in the future for one black man, or even a half dozen, to tower above the crowd as *the* black leader or leaders.

Politics offers a perfect example of the broadening of black leadership. There was a time when Adam Clayton Powell and Bill Dawson were the total of black leadership in Congress. Today most blacks probably cannot name all the black members of Congress. The number of black elected officials in the South has risen from just seventy-five in 1965 to almost six hundred today.

Yes, we mourn the passing of great men like Robinson. But we must not despair. New leaders and a new day are coming.

59

Former President Harry S. Truman is dead. Black Americans aged forty or older will mourn with special sadness, for they know that it was this "little guy" from Missouri who first put the White House on the side of black dignity and black equality.

On a January day twenty-six years ago Harry Truman invited fifteen distinguished Americans to the White House. He told of his outrage at repeated violence against Negroes, especially GIs returning from war. "I want our Bill of Rights implemented in fact," Truman said and he commissioned those fifteen Americans to tell him how.

Months later that committee stunned the nation with a massive report documenting the discrimination, abuse, brutalizations visited upon America's minorities. The committee's report, entitled "To Secure These Rights," called for a bold legislative program to guarantee civil rights and opportunities to black people.

Despite political danger, Harry Truman responded with equal boldness. On February 2, 1948, he sent a special message to Congress calling for a civil rights division of the Justice Department, the strengthening of civil rights statutes, federal protection against lynching, better protection of the right to vote, a federal Fair Employment Practices Commission, a ban on racial discrimination in interstate transportation, home rule for the District of Columbia, statehood for Hawaii and Alaska, and more self-government for other U.S. Territories.

Mr. Truman lived to see all of those goals reached, except home rule for the District of Columbia.

Harry Truman took his stand for civil rights in the face of political peril. Henry Wallace had defected on the left, and angry Dixiecrats would desert him on the right. But the little man from Missouri chose to do what he knew was right.

When J. Strom Thurmond, then governor of South Carolina, walked out of the 1948 Democratic convention in anger over the civil rights plank, a newsman said to him, "Why are you walking out? All Truman is doing is following the Roosevelt platform."

"I know," Thurmond replied, "but that S.O.B. Truman really means it."

We say farewell to Mr. Truman in gratitude for the rights black people struggle to retain these days. And we hope prayerfully that this nation may soon again have a leader of his principles and his guts.

60

It was six years ago that Dr. Martin Luther King, Jr., was slain in Memphis. Even at the time of his death some of the magic seemed to have leaked out of his movement. Angry blacks were denouncing his philosophy of non-violence. And Dr. King himself seemed to be groping for new directions, for new techniques with which to achieve black liberation.

I first met the young Dr. King in Montgomery, Alabama, in the early hours of the Montgomery bus boycott. I was impressed immediately by his pragmatic sense of politics. He knew the art of the possible, and he had an acute facility for saying just the right thing at the right time. He said just the things to make Alabama's advocates of segregation look like fools and to make himself a household word.

The Montgomery boycott succeeded. But let us not delude ourselves into believing that Gandhian tactics of nonviolence caused those Dixiecrat racists to knuckle under. It was a Supreme Court decision that finally gave Dr. King and his colleagues victory.

But the important truth is that Dr. King had been able to provoke change and carry the system with him. He dragged along the courts, the White House, most of the nation's media, the church leaders. There was evidence that he profoundly altered "the establishment."

But many months before his death a group of self-styled militants challenged Dr. King's leadership. Stokely Carmichael, Rap Brown and others were saying to hell with "the system." They talked mostly about what they intended to burn down.

Some students of Dr. King say that pressures from these self-styled militants forced him to change his style. They say he felt forced to adopt some of the angry rhetoric that became so popular among young blacks, even though he sensed that wild rhetoric and senseless violence would only infuriate and militarize oppressive forces within "the establishment" that he had half won over.

We know the result. The forces of hatred, bigotry, oppression did rise up. Dr. King was slain. This country was thrown into a "white backlash" that dominates this nation even today.

Some say Dr. King had given up on reforming "the

system" at the time of his death. They say he wanted a total reconstruction of this society. Others say this talk was just rhetoric to preserve his position of leadership.

I don't know who is right. I do know that I welcome the day when another leader emerges who has Dr. King's sense for doing and saying the right thing at the right time.

61

Lyndon Baines Johnson's body lies a-molding in a grave in his beloved Texas. The funeral tears have dried and the aches have gone out of all but a few hearts.

So now, quietly, I can tell you a little story about how Johnson taught me a new lesson about prejudice. He taught me not to judge a man on what part of the country he comes from, just as you and I don't want people to judge us on the basis of racial background.

When I went to the State Department in 1961 I had never met Lyndon Johnson. I was puzzled when he, as Vice-President, asked me to accompany him on a round-the-world mission for President Kennedy.

I shall never forget the sultry day in the Philippines when Johnson poked a finger in my chest and said: "Mr. Roe-ann, one of these days you're gonna discover that I'm a goddam sight more liberal than most of these so-called liberals you've been cottoning up to."

I had my doubts. After all, as a congressman from Texas, Johnson had supported Jim Crow. But later in the trip something happened to give me special insight into Johnson's character.

About 2 A.M. one weary morning in Saigon, Johnson's aide Horace Busby and I were struggling to finish a speech that Johnson was to deliver at 10 A.M., when into the room strolled the Vice-President in brown-and-white pajamas. He had come to ask *me* if he should buy Perle Mesta's house in Washington.

"They know Kennedy's rich," he said. "Now, are those vultures in the press gonna start writing about 'the millionaire Administration' if I buy that house?"

I was about to say, *"Buy the house,"* when he stopped me with a warning that he hadn't told me fully why he wanted my advice.

Then Johnson explained that a fellow senator had talked him into joining the snooty Chevy Chase club in a suburb of Washington. Lady Bird had tried to give a party for Lynda Bird when the club demanded to see her guest list. Johnson recalled that they told Lady Bird: "No, we don't discriminate. We just want to make sure you don't invite any Negroes or too many Jews."

The Vice-President bristled and said to me: "I told Lady Bird that I was gonna buy her a goddam house where when she gets ready to give a party she don't have to give nobody her guest list.

"Now, Mr. Roe-ann," he asked, "do you think I ought to buy Perle Mesta's house?"

Johnson bought The Elms, Mrs. Mesta's marvelous house. And he invited blacks, Jews and whomever he pleased to his parties.

I learned in that wee-hours conversation in Saigon that he was more than just another Texas politician. I was not at all surprised that when he became President, he put on the books the most comprehensive civil rights legislation in the nation's history.

Lyndon Johnson was not just a friend of black people. He was a friend of *people*—and justice, and decency. And we shall miss him.

62

Many of you were probably shocked to hear on radio and television that Roy Wilkins had been forced out as executive director of the NAACP. Then you were puzzled to learn that while Wilkins has been under attack, the board really hadn't fired him.

What the devil's happening at the NAACP? you ask. I'll tell you.

Roy Wilkins is seventy-two years old. He has been the NAACP kingpin for three decades. The board chairman, Bishop Stephen G. Spottswood, and one of Wilkins' key aides, Henry Lee Moon, are both in their seventies. A lot of people think they all ought to retire and let younger, more vigorous people lead the quest for black dignity and liberation. But Wilkins makes it clear that he is not about to retire, so it is inevitable that some NAACP leaders will go on trying to force him out.

But there's more to Wilkins' problems than his age. The NAACP has fallen into that God-forbidden zone where no one loves it enough or hates and fears it enough to keep people believing that it is vital. Thus NAACP membership has lagged, and questions arise across the land as to whether the NAACP is still relevant to the needs and wishes of black people. This is quite a comedown from those days in the fifties when blacks swore by the NAACP, and Southern whites cursed at it.

I remember traveling across the South right after the 1954 Supreme Court decision outlawing segregated schools. Georgia's Senator Herman Talmadge said: "The most accomplished and professional race-baiters in the world are the spokesmen for the NAACP." The governor of South Carolina, George Bell Timmerman, Jr., said: "The colored officers of the NAACP are professional agitators."

A standard joke in those days was about the white industrialist who would gladly hire a spook to sit by the door "If you just don't sic the NAACP on me."

The NAACP began to have image problems when the Rev. Martin Luther King strode into the limelight with boycotts, marches, demonstrations. And then Stokely Carmichael, Rap Brown and other self-styled "militants" grabbed headlines with rhetoric about "Whitey" that Wilkins considered foolishly counterproductive.

The press started speaking of Wilkins and the NAACP as "moderate," and that can be a curse at a time when many blacks are jobless, directionless and virtually hopeless. But let the record be clear: Roy Wilkins has never been a moderate in the sense that he compromised the rights of black people.

He deserves only the commendation of a grateful people. He ought to retire to roaring cheers. It would be a tragedy if he were to hang on doggedly until forced out.

Good leadership is essential to black survival. Only fools fail to exercise their right to select their leaders.

But let us face the fact that "leaders" cannot do everything for us. Personal responsibility is absolutely essential if we are to ease the many problems of the black family . . .

63

Senator Edward Brooke, the only black member of the United States Senate, became the first Republican senator to ask publicly for the resignation of the President. Brooke told a nationwide TV audience that Mr. Nixon had lost the capacity to govern and ought to resign for the good of the country.

Meanwhile, black Congressman Charles B. Rangel of New York City reported that his office was flooded by mail demanding the impeachment of Mr. Nixon. Those developments suggested that blacks more than any other group are hoping that the Watergate scandals will produce the ouster of Richard Nixon. But some new figures from the Census Bureau about black voting in 1972 suggests that black political outrage comes a little late.

Senator Barry Goldwater, the conservative Republican from Arizona, says his mail is running 10 to 1 in favor of impeachment of President Nixon. It is not surprising, then, that Rangel should report more than four thousand letters from his constituents, with 99 per cent in favor of impeachment.

"The overall picture is clear," Rangel said. "The people of East Harlem, Harlem, and the upper West Side are fed up with the President's evasions, lies, and obstruction of justice."

Rangel says black people want Mr. Nixon impeached because of "his failure to stop inflation, his insensitivity to the needs of the poor, and his lack of commitment to improve the status of minorities ..."

These black demands are understandable. But one must ask black Americans: "Where were you with all your political outrage when the people went to the polls in 1968 and 1972?" Impeaching a President is infinitely more difficult than refusing to vote for him in the first place!

The Census Bureau reports that in 1968, when Mr. Nixon won a razor-thin victory over Hubert H. Humphrey, a mere 57.9 per cent of blacks over twenty-one bothered to vote. That means that about 5 million black adults loafed around the pool halls and taverns, or generally sat on their cans and didn't bother to cast ballots that could have changed the course of American history.

And who can doubt that many of these nonvoters are today screaming loudest for the resignation or impeachment of Mr. Nixon? And may I add that the black voting record was even worse in 1972 than in 1968. The percentage of voting-age blacks who actually cast ballots fell to a shameful 54.6 per cent.

It is perfectly proper that blacks, like all other Americans, should sound off about the Watergate scandals. It is heartening that Harlem blacks care enough to write thousands of letters to their congressman. But blacks and the country will be better off if black outrage is expressed at election time. In politics as in other areas of life, an ounce of prevention is worth a pound of cure.

There used to be a mediocre television program called *Get Smart*. Black Americans could adopt that title as a motto.

We are protest-oriented, but we lack knowledge of the things about which we need most to protest.

Take social security—prize product of Franklin D. Roosevelt's New Deal. It is not a total blessing for poor Americans—especially black Americans . . .

64

We now have some major improvements in social security benefits. And along with it, a hefty increase in the social security payroll tax. A lot of Americans are screaming about the unfairness of it all. And no one ought to scream louder than black Americans.

Let me make it clear that I support social security. But I am an outspoken critic of the way we finance it. My dismay is all the greater when I see millions of blacks putting big money into a system from which they will collect relatively little—because of early death.

In case you don't know it, they've been raising the

amount deducted from your payroll check with shocking frequency lately. The result is that the social security tax is now the second biggest raiser of federal revenues—after the personal income tax. More money is siphoned off through the payroll tax than is collected in income taxes from all the corporations of America.

More disturbing is the truth that the social security tax is one of the most unfair on the books. It has no relationship to ability to pay. You sweat, work two jobs, to earn $13,200 a year. So $772 is deducted from your paychecks. Across town is a doctor, lawyer, radio commentator who earns $100,000 a year. All he pays is the same $772 social security tax you pay.

No group carries a higher burden, relatively, than blacks because so few of them earn more than the $13,200 which will soon be the top amount tapped for social security. What few black people realize is that life expectancy for a thirty-two-year-old black man today is about sixty years, as compared with sixty-seven for a similar white man. This means that the average white worker will have several years to draw social security, but the black man very few.

White workers claim they are supporting welfare payments for poor blacks, but they never entertain the truth that blacks are supporting the social security payments for whites.

Senator Gaylord Nelson of Wisconsin is fighting to change our system of financing social security. He wants the burden removed from those least able to pay.

Instead of the payroll tax that cheats the working man, Nelson wants to wipe out the tax loopholes. He says that if we ended the super-fast depreciation that is a bonanza to business, and strengthened the requirement that all high-income people pay a decent tax no matter how many loopholes they find, the Treasury could raise an extra $42 billion in the next few years. That would pay for most of the new social security benefits.

But the laws will never change until you wake up to the truth—and complain as bitterly and loudly as you know how.

> And speaking of retirement, how many street protests have you seen by young people angry at the way aged blacks are left in want and degradation?

65

It's tough enough to be black in America. To be old and black is to carry a double burden. It means you face double discrimination. It means that chances are 50-50 you're living in poverty. It means you're likely to be ill-housed and ill-fed, and to receive inadequate medical care.

About 1.6 million American blacks are sixty-five years old and over. More than half of them still live in the South, although the largest single concentration is in New York City.

Actually, if you're black, you don't have as good a chance to reach a ripe old age as you do if you're white. The average life span of a black man is about sixty years, compared to sixty-seven years for a white man. The average black woman lives sixty-seven years, versus seventy-two for a white woman.

But as things stand now, that shorter life may be a blessing of sorts, for if you're an elderly black, your chances of being poor are double those of an elderly white. A special Senate committee reported a few years ago that "the non-white elderly appear to suffer from deeper extremes of impoverishment. They reflect all aspects of the poverty syndrome—poor health, dilapidated housing, malnourishment, limited education, transportation difficulties and absence of vitally needed services." Unfortunately, not much seems to be done about this. For example, only 3 per cent of federally subsidized housing projects for the aged are for blacks.

Not having enough money or food is not new to most aged blacks. They've lived that way all their lives. Denied adequate education and training, they've never been able to build up savings for old age. But even so, these conditions seem worse when one grows older because additional problems arise and some of the hardships you could shrug off or endure when you were young become more difficult when you're old.

Another trauma for blacks is pointed out in *Ebony* magazine by Dr. Jacquelyne Jackson of Duke University's center for the study of aging and human development. She notes that older blacks today no longer enjoy the role of respected family sage and elder which they once were given.

Still, aging blacks do have a couple of things going for them. Along with Jews, they are the ethnic group in which elderly parents are most likely to be living with children. And because they've lived through difficult times before, they find it easier to accept the hardships of old age than do elderly persons who have never known adversity.

What can be done to help the growing number of older people in our midst?

The biggest problem of the elderly is money—or lack of it. One old person out of every four is living below the poverty line. Among blacks the figure is one out of two. They have been caught in the squeeze between a fixed income and rising costs.

An important step was taken to ease the situation last year when the social security law was changed to provide automatic increases in benefits when the cost of living goes up more than 3 per cent a year. This will go into effect in 1975.

In the meantime, we should find ways to give property-tax relief to the elderly. Wisconsin has pioneered one plan. It provides that when property taxes reach a predetermined percentage of an elderly family's income, then all taxes above that cutoff point are refunded by the state.

Another way to aid older men and women is to find some kind of work for them. This would provide extra income, and it would furnish a big psychological boost, letting them know they still belong and are useful. That, say psychologists, can be as potent a tonic as any vitamin pill.

Some programs already exist. Senior AIDES assigns the aged to schools and day-care centers. Foster Grandparents pays low-income grandparents to care for underprivileged kids. The Executive Service Corps uses retired executives' managerial skills in developing nations.

In the area of health, we should not be so quick to relegate older citizens to the "senility heap." Doctors tell us that what we think of as unavoidable senility often involves psychological and physical problems that can be treated.

In her book on the aged, Simone de Beauvoir asks a haunting question: "What should a society be like so that in his old age a man can remain a man?"

She answers simply: "He must always be treated like a man." This means respect for all people—all through life. And when a man or woman does reach old age, adequate income, housing, medical care are certainly important, but these people need something more if the years are to be "golden." Most of all, they need to be cared about.

The aged face one crushing burden that besets blacks of all ages: the ravages of illness, disease, general poor health.

They all live—and die—with the problem of getting adequate medical care at a price black people can afford. Not only do we blacks not fight hard enough for decent medical care; many of us don't even know what ails us—or kills us.

66

Some of the best medical care in the world is available here in the United States—for those who can pay for it. But for millions of poor and near-poor, the excellence of American health care doesn't really mean much. Medical miracles are beyond their grasp. They live instead in the midst of illness and death.

The disparity of medical care in America is appalling.

Among the poor, and especially among nonwhites, there is a serious shortage of doctors and hospitals, and poor distribution of those that are available. This produces some shocking statistics:

• For every two white babies who die in the first four weeks of life, three nonwhite babies die. And after those first four weeks, a nonwhite baby has only one-third the chance that a white baby has of celebrating its first birthday.

Statistics like these are turned into human dramas in a report from Meharry Medical School, which turns out almost half of America's black doctors.

• A six-year-old black girl in the South dies of diphtheria because her mother never heard of inoculation against the disease.

• A black mother gets no prenatal care. She has had an inadequate diet most of her life. Her child is born prematurely and is mentally retarded. The mother herself dies in childbirth.

• A young black boy has an ear infection. To take him to the clinic, his mother has to take all five of her children on two buses, then wait most of the day to get a doctor to look at her son. As a result, she doesn't go back. The boy becomes deaf in one ear.

Heart disease, arthritis, mental illness, high blood pressure, visual troubles. All are more common among the poor. Twenty-nine per cent of those people who make less than $2,000 a year have chronic conditions that limit their activity. Less than 8 per cent of those making over $7,000 are handicapped in that way.

I could go on and on. The net result is more than physical impairment. Family stability is damaged, earning power is reduced, the chances for education are lost, and the vicious cycle of poverty is continued.

67

Eleven per cent of the population of the United States is black. Only 2 per cent of the doctors are black. This disparity helps explain the situation of poor medical care for the poor and blacks. But there is more to the problem than just numbers. Medical care also depends on how and where scarce skills are used.

The United States has 1 physician for every 600 people in the general population; but there is only 1 black physician for every 3,500 black people.

Negro dentists are even more scarce. The ratio of black dentists to the black population is 1 to 11,500, as compared to 1 to 1,900 in the overall population.

The problem is most serious in the South and in urban areas. In 1970 Mississippi had only 100 Negro physicians, surgeons and dentists among a black population of 950,000. By comparison, 1,350,000 white Mississippians were served by 1,800 professionals. In many big-city ghettos and poverty areas, not a single doctor has hung out his shingle.

Most of the black physicians come from two predominantly black medical schools—Meharry in Nashville, Tennessee, and Howard in Washington, D.C. There is an urgent need to step up their enrollment, and to expand the number of black students in the nation's other 100-plus medical schools.

There has been an increase recently in minority-group students admitted to medical school, but many do not get degrees. Medical school deans suggest that the higher drop-out rate results from previous educational experiences and poor study habits. Students themselves have asked for more tutorial help. Another aid for getting more enrolled would be greater financial assistance for scholarships and loans.

Merely increasing numbers will not be enough. Also important is using the scarce supply and skills as effectively as possible.

One program pushed by Meharry is comprehensive community medicine. Under this, doctors and dentists work with a variety of professionals—social workers, public health nurses, nutritionists, medical specialists. They form a health team, which looks at the patient from many points of view—his education, family, housing, job, etc. In this way, the team not only treats illness but tries to get at the roots of it.

Community medicine is hailed as the most effective, least expensive way to deliver health care for all.

But all efforts toward improvement of medical care for blacks are eventually frustrated by racism . . .

68

Discrimination in medical care has long been one of the ugliest chapters of racial discrimination in America. Within easy memory of many who listen to this program are the cases of blacks dying on the sidewalk because an ambulance for "whites only" would not transport them to a hospital. Many have been the cases of blacks in desperate need of medical attention being turned away by white hospitals.

Such grossly nauseating episodes are virtually unheard of these days, but don't you believe for a moment that racial discrimination has disappeared from medical care. In fact, Representative Charles B. Rangel, the New York Democrat, is livid over what he calls the "segregation of the sick right under the nose of the Federal Government."

Rangel is a member of the House Subcommittee on Civil Rights and Constitutional Rights of the Judiciary Committee. This subcommittee has been holding hearings to determine whether federal funds are being withheld, as required by law, from facilities that practice racial discrimination.

Rangel charges that "Hospitals are openly maintaining segregated wards and rooms and are allowed to get away with the flimsiest of excuses that this segregation arises out of economic circumstance."

Rangel charges that the Nixon Administration simply refuses to enforce the law so as to ensure that such programs as Medicare and Medicaid do not work as supporters of injustice.

Rangel is especially irate over testimony taken from witnesses from Aiken, South Carolina. These witnesses testified that doctors and others who are filling bank accounts with federal money are allowed to impose their own ideas of morality on those needing medical attention.

Some black women seeking prenatal care and delivery of their babies have been told: "You don't get any medical care unless you agree to be sterilized. You don't need any more children."

The truth may be that some of the women don't need to have any more babies. But medical people operating on government funds must never be in a position to coerce black people, or any other people, into sterilization.

Rangel admits that he is frustrated because this is not a situation where he might remedy the situation by introducing a new law. The laws already on the books are clear. "But how," he asks, "does one force the government to obey the law of the land?"

The simple reality is that whatever the party in power, Presidents usually enforce the laws they truly believe in. They ignore those laws that clash with their own prejudices and predilections.

This is why, in a democracy, the first line of protection is the political process. You stay informed, work to elect the politicians who are committed to racial justice. If you don't vote and don't care, crying later is a useless exercise.

However inclined we may be to gripe about discrimination in medical care, we cannot afford to ignore the care, knowledge, research and other resources that are available.

Blacks cannot blame Whitey for their failure to learn something about those diseases that take a special toll of Negroes . . .

69

Go to just about any black funeral home, or sit in on a wake, and you'll hear a dialogue that goes something like this:

"Wasn't it shocking that Cousin Bertha died of a stroke? Why, she'd been the picture of health, except for her high blood pressure."

"Yeah, my Brother Bill died in the same surprising way. He had a heart attack when he'd never complained about a thing except his high blood pressure."

There are a lot of Cousin Berthas and Brother Bills in black America—mostly because not enough black Americans know that high blood pressure is the number-one killer of black people.

If you suffer from high blood pressure—the doctor may call it hypertension—you can be sure that you are in danger of a disease of the heart, the brain, the kidney. But the pathetic possibility is that you may be among the 10 million Americans who are afflicted with high blood pressure but don't know it.

Then there are 10 million who suffer and know it, but only half of them are receiving long-term care from physicians. And half of those seeing doctors are getting lousy treatment, the experts say.

The shame is that good treatment exists for high blood pressure, but too few people get it. So diseases flowing from hypertension are among the most neglected in this country.

It may or may not surprise you that it is blacks who

suffer most. Blacks make up only 11 per cent of the population, yet 25 per cent of the cardiovascular diseases affect black Americans. In the South a black is three times as likely to fall victim to a hypertensive disease as a white person.

Dr. Howard W. Kenney, head of a thirteen-state medical region for the Veterans Administration, says that between the ages of twenty-five to forty-four, high blood pressure kills 15.5 times as many black males as whites, and 17 times as many black females.

Doctors are not sure what causes high blood pressure. Some suspect that eating a lot of salt, which is common in this country, is one cause. But why is high blood pressure so common among American blacks when it is not so prevalent in Africa? Some medical men think that the pressures of surviving in a hostile society dominated by whites has a lot to do with it.

The Secretary of Health, Education and Welfare recently announced that the federal government is giving priority to fighting hypertension. Some cynical blacks are saying that a first cure would be for the government to give black people a fair break at jobs and housing.

But more than cynicism and anger are required from black people. This is one area where they can truly help themselves.

Remember that old cliché that you hear so often: "What you don't know won't hurt you!"? Well, high blood pressure is an area where what you don't know could kill you.

70

Guess who flirts most dangerously with the undertaker—a fat woman with high blood pressure who smokes and eats a lot of fats and sweets.

Right there you have the answer, and part of the cure, to the problem of so many black women—and men—dying from diseases caused by high blood pressure.

The number-one medical problem for American blacks is not cancer or much-publicized sickle-cell anemia. It is high blood pressure, an ailment that most black victims don't even know they have.

Do you want to live long enough to have grandchildren, or collect some of those social security checks that you pay for every week? Then you'd better get checked as to whether you have high blood pressure.

The Veterans Administration recently announced that 16 of its 167 hospitals are starting in-depth screening and follow-up of all patients for hypertension. Some 17 per cent of all VA patients are blacks, so this is a good way to start fighting the disease.

If you're not a VA patient, go to your private doctor, your public hospital or clinic. Raise hell till someone somewhere will examine you and tell you if you have high blood pressure.

If you do suffer from hypertension, face up to this grim fact: you are a pretty good bet to drop dead from a heart attack or a stroke if you are obese, you smoke a lot or you follow a high-cholesterol diet—meaning lots of fat meat, milk, butter, eggs, lard.

That's a mean truth. Because obesity is common throughout this society, but being overweight is particularly prevalent among black women. Another simple truth is that poor people eat lots of fat. High-protein, low-carbohydrate diets cost more. Poor people (and that means many black people) eat what they can get their hands on today, for they can never be sure what tomorrow will bring.

Obviously, then, we lift a death sentence from a lot of black people when we lift them out of poverty. So you had better scream and shout for better job programs and anti-poverty programs. They mean life and death to black people.

Don't just blame white discrimination and oppression for your high blood pressure and resign yourself to dying young. Even on a limited income you can follow a healthy diet—if only you will follow good advice.

71

A rather delicate question for the women who listen to "Black Perspectives": Did you have a Pap smear, or an examination of the breasts, in 1973?

This is not an impertinent bit of meddling. It's the query of a journalist who is disturbed by medical reports that more and more black women are dying of cancer.

Dr. Mildred I. Clarke recently wrote in *Essence* magazine of alarming statistics from the Howard University School of Medicine showing more and more black women dying of cancer of the breast and/or the genital area. Dr. Clarke cited an American Cancer Society estimate of 43,000 new cases of cancer of the uterus in 1972, with 12,000 deaths.

Cancer of the cervix is a deadly killer of black women. No one knows exactly why, any more than they know other answers to questions about this dread disease. But here are some statistics and facts that you had better keep in mind.

The Pap test is a remarkable lifesaver. No woman can discover for herself early symptoms of cervical cancer. But a gynecologist, or the family doctor, can—with a painless, simple examination. Early detection is saving a lot of women's lives.

Statistics show that circumcised men have less cancer of the penis than uncircumcised men. Doctors say that Jewish and Moslem women have a very low incidence of cancer of the cervix. Some think that being married to a circumcised man may be a factor in avoiding cancer of the uterus.

Another interesting statistic is that single women who have never had children report a low incidence of cancer of the cervix. The record seems to be clear that women who marry, or are exposed sexually, at very early ages are flirting with cancer of the cervix. So are those who have sexual relationships with numerous partners, or have too many babies, or have babies at a very young age.

No doctor anywhere knows enough about cancer or how to prevent it. So obviously this reporter is not playing medicine man. I am simply warning of the dreadful toll that cancer is taking among black women.

I am passing along the good news that a simple annual checkup could save many thousands of lives because cancer of the cervix is almost 100 per cent curable if it is diagnosed early.

Black is beautiful, dear woman, but only when you have the good sense to stay healthy—and alive.

72

Suppose you were asked to name the leading communicable disease in America today, not counting the common cold. What would you answer? Measles? Mumps? Chicken pox? If you said any of those, you'd be wrong. Right behind the common cold among communicable diseases is venereal disease. V.D. Syphilis and gonorrhea.

Venereal diseases infect more persons than measles, tuberculosis, hepatitis, whooping cough and encephalitis combined. V.D. has reached epidemic proportions and threatens the health, even the lives, of hundreds of thousands of Americans. There's a widespread assumption that V.D. was almost wiped out with those handy penicillin shots and helpful how-not-to-do-it movies for GIs. Don't you believe it.

More than 1.5 million Americans have gonorrhea. That's half a million more than a decade ago. Another 75,000 are known to be infected with syphilis, and doctors believe that as many as a million persons may have the disease but don't know it.

V.D. strikes more often in ghetto areas, but nobody is immune. Perhaps most startling is the number of young people who are infected. There are an estimated 300,000 cases among teen-agers—three times the national average for gonorrhea, two times the average for syphilis.

The reasons for the epidemic vary. One of the main ones is lack of knowledge. A lot of people still think you get V.D. from toilet seats or kissing. Another is The Pill, which has led to a decrease in the use of condoms—and increased promiscuity, some say.

Venereal disease can be cured if treated promptly and properly, but if not, it can be very serious. Syphilis can cripple, cause mental deterioration, blindness, even death. Gonorrhea is less damaging, but it can leave victims sterile.

How can we combat this growing epidemic? One of the keys is through education campaigns involving parents, schools, community agencies. Also, we need money—for research, public-health caseworkers and clinics. And we need cooperation from doctors in reporting cases.

The ultimate key to halting the V.D. epidemic is you. If you think you have V.D., see a doctor. If you think someone in your family does, get them to a doctor. See that the person who gave it to you sees a doctor. Sex is too nice to be abused with stupidity and indifference.

73

If you live in an old house, in one of America's central cities, and you have children, you had better worry about lead poisoning.

The federal government says that lead poisoning is more prevalent among children aged one to six than polio was before development of the Salk vaccine. Poor children, minority-group children, are especially susceptible to this ailment that is sometimes called "the silent epidemic."

The Joint Center for Political Studies in Washington, D.C., has put out a disturbing report on a frightful affliction called "plumbism"—commonly known as lead poisoning. The Center reports that every year 200 children die, 800 suffer severe brain damage, 3,000 suffer moderate-to-severe brain damage and 16,000 require medical treatment because of lead poisoning. Annually some 400,000 youngsters experience increases in the level of lead in their blood that could lead to serious medical problems.

What problems? Blindness, mental retardation, cerebral palsy, kidney diseases, behavior disorders, convulsion—and even death. Any one or several of these may afflict the victim of lead poisoning.

The terrible thing about lead poisoning is that there is nothing mysterious about it, the way polio used to be a mystery, or cancer or cystic fibrosis involve mysteries today.

Children's lead poisoning is a simple, tragic product of parental ignorance and carelessness of landlord greed and indifference. This ailment is sometimes called "ghetto malaria" because this country's ghettos are full of houses whose walls are coated with peeling, lead-bearing paint that was put on more than three decades ago.

Some children pick up paint chips from the walls and ceilings and eat them out of curiosity. Doctors say other children are afflicted with something called "pica," a strong craving for eating nonfood objects. Every paint chip eaten builds the level of lead in the child's system. Just one thumbnail-sized chip eaten every day for three months can seriously poison a child.

If your child eats enough leaded paint to suffer moderate brain damage, it can mean special care and training for perhaps ten years, at a cost of $17,500. If your child suffers severe brain damage, he or she will probably spend a life-time in an institution.

Obviously, then, you want to protect your child from lead poisoning.

74

So you've noticed the paint chips falling off your walls and ceiling into your baby's crib. You think your child has been eating paint. And you are worried.

There is no way you can just look at your child, or study symptoms of his illness, and determine whether you have a case of lead poisoning. Even doctors sometimes mistake a dangerous case of lead poisoning for a routine childhood illness.

So your child suffers from a stomach ache, weakness, constipation, sleeplessness, vomiting, anemia, headache, irritability, loss of weight, loss of appetite. These are all minor childhood complaints, but they could be symptoms of lead poisoning. More severe symptoms would be dizziness, staggering, paralysis, convulsion and pains in the joints, according to a report compiled by the Joint Center for Political Studies.

This report suggests that if you suspect your child has been eating paint chips, let a doctor check the level of lead in your child's blood. That may seem a bit troublesome, but it isn't nearly as much trouble as a funeral—or caring for a handicapped child the rest of your life.

You see, lead poisoning is curable if caught in time.

The ideal thing, of course, is to see that your child is not exposed to poisonous paint chips. Don't be too timid, or proud, to complain to authorities if paint is falling off your walls and ceilings.

Congress has set up a Bureau of Community Environmental Management in the Department of Health, Education and Welfare just to protect your child from lead poisoning. That bureau has a cool $7.5 million to spend this year. It is up to you to see that it is spent in ways that protect your children.

You can do a lot to erase this scourge of lead poisoning among children. Demand screening programs in the "lead belts" of the ghettos so medical men can determine which children need immediate treatment. *Insist* that good treatment is made readily available.

Band together and form some economic and political power so you can force landlords to renovate housing that is full of poisoned paint.

Meanwhile, it wouldn't hurt if you read the full report on childhood lead poisoning. Drop a note to the Joint Center for Political Studies, 1426 H Street, N.W., Washington, D.C. 20005.

The child you'll save is one you'll love.

75

"What's all this talk about sickle cell anemia?" the black woman asked me. "Isn't it just another cheap way to woo Negro votes?" This woman added what a lot of black people have been saying: they have never known a single person who died from sickle cell anemia, so how come all the recent publicity about it?

My answer to that woman was that in a political year there is politics in everything. However, sickle cell anemia is a terrible disease that attacks blacks, and a campaign to combat it is long overdue.

Medical men say some fifty thousand black Americans suffer from sickle cell anemia, a dread disease for which there is no known cure—and a disease that afflicts black people almost exclusively.

The disease goes back to Africa, more than a thousand years ago, where red blood cells began to take on a sickle-like shape that somehow made them less vulnerable to malaria. But as malaria became less a problem it became obvious that the sickle cells were killers themselves. These sickled cells are unable to carry the oxygen needed by various parts of the human body.

So the fifty thousand black Americans and the Africans who have the disease are often wracked with pain. They have swollen hands and feet; they fail to grow normally; their sexual development is delayed; their legs become abnormally long for the size of their bodies. They are prone to infections, with many of them dying of pneumonia. Half of all sickle cell anemia patients die before they are twenty-one, and it is unusual to have a victim live until forty.

The people who actually suffer from the disease are only the surface of the problem. An estimated 2.5 million black Americans—or one out of every ten—carries the sickle cell *trait*. If one trait carrier marries another, danger lurks in the production of children.

If two carriers of the sickle cell have four children, the odds are that one child will get the disease, one child will carry the sickle cell gene recessively, and two will have normal hemoglobin.

This raises the point that a person with the sickle cell trait might want to be sure not to marry another carrier of this gene. Or if two such people do marry, they will want to ponder seriously the risks of having children.

The cure for sickle cell anemia is unknown. Yet it is easy to learn whether you carry the trait. A simple, fast screening test costs only five to fifteen cents. Young blacks would be wise to take the sickle cell test. Unfortunately, this disease, like too many other things, is ensnared in racial passions and politics.

76

The current campaign against sickle cell anemia has aroused deep distrust and suspicion in parts of the black community. Blacks ask why the disease was known for more than sixty years before the government and organized medicine decided to fight it. Cries of "genocide" have even arisen in the most militant, most suspicious sectors of the black community.

Senator Edward M. Kennedy, chairman of the Senate health subcommittee, has told it like it is regarding the sixty-year delay in attacking sickle cell anemia. He says that cystic fibrosis is six times as rare as sickle cell anemia, but cystic fibrosis occurs principally in white people, so "astronomical" sums are allocated for research on and treatment of that disease. But "sickle cell anemia has been neglected and ignored like most other conditions that affect only black people," Kennedy added.

Finally the federal government is allocating money and great medical centers are devoting their talent to research on the sickle cell. Yet blacks in some places like the National Institutes of Health have called for "massive resistance" to sickle cell programs.

Some blacks resent the fact that whites are organizing and directing programs that deal almost exclusively with the health of black people. Some blacks fear that the medical histories put in personnel records of blacks who are screened for sickle cell will somehow be used against blacks.

The fact is that a person who simply carries the trait goes about work and life just as normally as anyone else. The only trouble would be if he or she produces children with someone who also carries the trait.

But the fear persists that personnel officers, insurance companies and others might discriminate against a black person simply because he carries the trait. Several instances of such discrimination have been documented.

Others who scream "genocide" carry their suspicions to the point of expressing fear that the government will use the sickle cell trait as an excuse to forbid black people to have babies.

Some of these fears are far-fetched. The truth that black people must accept is that sickle cell anemia is a horrible disease that can be prevented if black people show a reasonable amount of care and concern.

If you have the sickle cell trait and marry someone who has it, you are going to prolong and multiply this disease if you have children. It is as simple as that—and you don't need whites or the government to tell you what to do. All you need do is make your own decision of whether you want to produce a child who suffers horribly, or whether you want to try to wipe out this wretched disease.

77

A mother tucks her five-month baby into his crib. He seems healthy and strong and he falls asleep quickly. But in the morning, when she goes to wake him, the baby is dead, and no one—not even the doctor—knows why.

Every year in America some 10,000 to 15,000 babies die during the night in this mysterious way. The tragedy is known as "sudden infant death syndrome," or crib death. Among infants between one month and one year old in the United States, it is the most frequent cause of death. One out of every 325 babies born alive in this country dies from crib death. And the percentage is even higher among the poor and blacks.

Crib death is one of medicine's most frustrating and

aggravating mysteries. It is not new. Some authorities think there are references to it in the Bible. A Scottish doctor wrote about it in a medical journal seventy-five years ago. But confusion and ignorance still exist. No cure, no prevention or protection has been found.

For a long time, crib death was blamed on smothering —either in bedclothes or under a mother's body. That idea has been shot down. So has the notion that viral infection is the cause. Some other possible factors which doctors are investigating include bacteria and the sleeping patterns of babies.

While they haven't pinpointed the cause, researchers have discovered some facts about the victims of crib death. The illness is significantly higher among blacks than whites— a rate of 4.6 cases pere 1,000 population, compared to 2.7. And it strikes boys more often than girls.

No family is safe. Deaths occur everywhere. But the poor are the most vulnerable, according to a Temple University doctor who has done extensive research. Clusters of cases of crib death have been found in slums and poor areas.

Because the child's death occurs so unexpectedly and without clues, parents sometimes are treated as criminal suspects by police, or they blame themselves. In extreme cases, the death of a child in this way has led to divorce or to psychiatric problems for the parents.

Such feelings or accusations of guilt—while understandable—are unwarranted. Dr. Abraham Bergman of Children's Orthopedic Hospital in Seattle, Washington, one of the experts in this field, says: "Crib death is neither predictable nor preventable. The divorces, the mental illness, the torment of unrelieved guilt are completely preventable by the humane handling of infant death cases."

It's sad enough that thousands of babies die each year from this mysterious ailment. There's no point in compounding the tragedy with callous treatment of parents.

78

So you're always screaming at your little boy to sit down and be quiet . . . to stop knocking things over . . . to get back to his homework. Or the teacher keeps sending notes that he's "a troublemaker" who's forever stirring up devilment. And he can't seem to pay attention to the lesson.

Your child probably suffers from hyperkinesis, a behavior disorder that afflicts millions of schoolchildren.

A California medical researcher *thinks* he's found a major reason for hyperactivity in children: it's those artificial flavors and colors that are in so many foods and beverages these days.

Just ten years ago only 2 per cent of California's schoolchildren were hyperactive. Now 20 to 25 per cent are reported to display behavior problems. What we used to call "Peck's little bad boy" is now so commonplace that many doctors virtually make a living treating children with allergy-control procedures, or with amphetamines, to calm them down. There has even been a lot of controversial talk about brain surgery to alter the behavior of "problem children."

Well, the problem may simply be that millions of children are victims of the chemicals used to produce some three thousand flavors and eleven basic synthetic colors that are so commonly used in drinks and food. Your child's breakfast cereal, soda pop, frozen waffles, pancake mix, hot dogs, luncheon meats and ice cream are all loaded with these artificial flavors and synthetic colors.

Ben Feingold, Chief Emeritus of the allergy department of the Kaiser-Permanente Medical Complex in San Francisco, has reported to several prominent medical groups that hyperactive children began to behave normally after he put them on a diet free of these chemicals. These same children reverted to hyperkinesis after violating the diet by taking even one bit or gulp of a chemically treated food or beverage.

Feingold pointed out that it is not just fad foods, or routine things that children like to eat or drink, that cause problems. A conscientious mother may give her child chewable vitamins, he pointed out, but even those vitamins contain chemicals that may diminish the child's attention span and ability to learn. Feingold even speculates that when a woman eats and drinks things loaded with chemical additives during her pregnancy, she may bequeath hyperkinesis to her child.

The Black Perspective here is quite simple. A lot of little black boys are singled out by teachers as hyperactive "problem" children. And we know that poor black kids eat and drink a lot of junk that is chock-full of additives that give phony flavors and colors.

If your child is too active for his own good, unable to concentrate on schoolwork, I can't guarantee you that his diet is his problem. There are many sources of hyperkinesis. But you would do well to put him on foods and drinks that are free of the suspect additives. Visit a clinic or talk to a doctor.

The child you help will more than ever be your own.

We all want our children to be born normal, to grow up in good health, to excel in their studies and to go on to life-long achievements that fill us with pride.

Unhappily, millions of poor Americans cannot even entertain such a dream. They can scarcely feed and clothe their children, let alone equip and prepare them to compete successfully in a highly technological, dog-eat-dog society.

In many instances, every child born in these families of poverty and ignorance is doomed to a life of misery—and the eventual production of more children who will become entrapped in the same vicious generation-to-generation cycle.

Thus the urging of birth control, family planning, contraception, abortion for poor adults. This has always aroused suspicions that whites wanted to solve the so-called Negro problem by wiping out all Negroes. Never have black fears and suspicions been greater.

79

In July 1972 the nation was shocked to learn that 430 black males in Alabama had been used as human guinea pigs by the Public Health Service.

Doctors trying to determine the effects of syphilis simply neglected for forty years to treat these infected men, many of whom knew only that they had "bad blood."

All this has produced a national furor over the abuse of poor, unknowing people in medical experiments. The Public Health Service drew 430 black men in Macon County, Alabama, into their syphilis experiment in 1932 with a promise of $50, hot meals and burial costs.

Even when penicillin became available as an easy cure for syphilis, the men went untreated. The researchers wanted to see the ravages of advanced syphilis. They saw. At least 28 and perhaps 107 of the men died directly because of syphilis. Another 100 or so were crippled by blindness, insanity and other effects.

When this so-called Tuskegee study was exposed last year, the Department of Health, Education and Welfare sought to make amends. It asked a special citizens panel to recommend what to do.

End the experiment and provide treatment for the known survivors, was the first recommendation. Incredibly, HEW bureaucrats argued for weeks that they had no authority to provide treatment—until HEW Secretary Caspar W. Weinberger personally ordered medical care to forestall a national hue and cry.

Meanwhile several Americans, including Senator James B. Allen of Alabama, have urged Congress to compensate the victims of this experiment and their survivors—up to a maximum of $25,000 per victim. The bill to provide compensation has languished in the Senate Judiciary Committee, chaired by Senator James Eastland of Mississippi.

Surely no less important than paying the survivors for their suffering is the erecting of safeguards to ensure that other humans are not used so cruelly in the future.

That special HEW panel wants the government to create a permanent national investigation board to monitor government research that uses human subjects. Such a board is vitally needed. Many a cancer victim undergoes chemotherapy without any knowledge as to the far-out nature or the extra hazards of some of the drugs being employed.

Those syphilis victims were treated as of little more consequence than 430 mice. This society can never tolerate that kind of cruelty—not even in the name of scientific advancement.

80

First we had the scandal of the so-called Tuskegee experiment—the using of black men as guinea pigs to determine the ravages of untreated syphilis. Now comes another scandal out of Alabama: the use of federal antipoverty funds for the sterilization of young black women without the apparent informed consent of their parents.

No doubt you have read or heard about twelve-year-old Mary Alice Relf and fourteen-year-old Minnie Relf, two Alabama girls who were sterilized in a federally supported family-planning clinic. The parents, Mr. and Mrs. Lonnie Relf, have filed a million-dollar lawsuit, claiming that they did not give their informed consent.

I shall not try that lawsuit on this "Black Perspectives" program, or even try to resolve all the conflicting testimony and evidence. But I do want to talk about the impact of this kind of scandal, and how it blinds poor black people to the truth about their own best interests.

Blacks have long been suspicious of white medicine

men where the reproductive organs are concerned. Black doctors tell me that it long was common practice in much of the Deep South for white doctors to do hysterectomies on black women when there was no medical need whatever to render them unable to have babies. The assumption was that whites had some kind of compulsion to limit the black population, whether to limit the number of potential black voters or to limit the number of blacks who might require welfare.

This is why many blacks become immediately hostile toward any white person who shows up preaching birth control or family planning. "Genocide" is the cry that goes up from the more militant blacks.

The cry takes on ominous new meaning when you get the federal government involved in the sterilization of twelve- and fourteen-year-old girls. It is a terribly frightening thing, this specter of the government deciding who shall be able to bear children. It conjures up nightmarish visions of the use of medicine and science to perpetrate some master-race theory. This we must stop—and we will.

But there are some truths about voluntary family planning that blacks cannot overlook. As we reject forced or devious sterilization programs, we ought not overlook this crucial truth: a retarded, hungry, neglected child makes a poor soldier in the fight for black liberation. The black couple is smart, then, to have only the number of children that it can support in a decently human environment.

The stupidity, the madness, of the Alabama case must not blind black Americans to the absolute necessity of voluntary restraints on the number of babies they bring into this crowded, polluted planet.

81

Now and then you hear reports of opposition in the ghettos to the distribution of birth-control devices or family planning information. A couple of years ago, black delegates walked out of a conference on population and environment.

The reasons behind these actions are similar. A number of blacks have doubts, reservations and suspicions about family planning. Some are legitimate, some irrational. But all are real.

When you start talking about birth control or family planning, you run into two big hangups among blacks and other minorities. One is that they have trouble seeing population as an overriding concern, especially when there are other things to worry about like where the next meal will come from or whether there'll be a job to go to tomorrow.

It's not hard to understand and sympathize with this feeling. But what should be kept in mind is that many of these personal and community problems are closely linked to population, and vice versa.

The Commission on Population Growth said in its final report—and I quote: "Unless we address our major domestic social problems in the short run—beginning with racism and poverty—we will not be able to resolve fully the question of population growth. And unless we can resolve the question of population growth, in the long run it not only will further aggravate our current problems, but may eventually dwarf them."

The second big hangup is the fear that population control is some kind of sinister plan devised by the majority to limit the power of minorities, or even to wipe them out. Genocide, in other words. This fear stems in part from growing nationalism and the belief that in numbers lies power, political or other. But before anyone runs out and urges black women to bear babies as fast as they can to help the cause, he should pause and consider a few sobering aspects.

It's not quantity that's most important. It's quality. What good are ten or twelve children if they're born into conditions under which they can't develop their full potential? Unwanted children, too many children, strain family budgets and create physical and psychological problems for both parents and children.

Doctors tell us that women are more likely to have premature children if they bear a lot of babies in rapid succession or keep on having them until a late age. And premature children are more likely to be retarded or otherwise handicapped. A mentally retarded child makes a poor soldier in the fight for racial equality.

When family-planning clinics and services are set up for minorities, they should be set up in a dignified, humane way, with people from the community actively involved. And along with offering contraceptives, society must provide good jobs, schools, homes.

When this happens, there is no reason why the poor should not—and will not—welcome these services.

82

Remember that old "yea—boo" game we used to play. Somebody would call out a piece of good news, like "We're all going on a picnic tomorrow," and everyone responded with a "yea." Then the leader would say, "But it's gonna rain." And back came a chorus of boos.

Well, something like that is going on now with the federal program for providing family-planning services to low-income women. Hopes are being raised with reports of how well it's working, then lowered with warnings that the whole thing may be wiped out for lack of money.

A study made for the Department of Health, Education and Welfare reports that more than 3 million low-income women in America have received family-planning services under federally subsidized programs. That means we're halfway toward the goal set by President Nixon of providing these services to all women who want them—whether they can pay or not.

The number of women helped has tripled since 1968, and the spending on these programs has increased from $10 million to $123 million. If federal and local support continues to grow at the same rate it has, then 6½ million women —the entire number estimated to be in need—will be served by 1975.

That news rates a hearty "yea." But now for the hooker: the whole program is in danger of being undermined by cutbacks in federal spending.

The Administration's proposed budget for fiscal 1974

would fund family planning only at the 1972 level. And there is concern among family-planning advocates that the government may try to set up a revenue-sharing plan which could further cripple the low-income program.

The loss would be an especially harsh blow to the many blacks and others who have been beneficiaries. These women come from socioeconomic groups which have relatively high rates of unwanted pregnancy and relatively high fertility rates. In the past, they have not always had knowledge of or access to the best methods of contraception. The federal program has made available, on a voluntary basis, the most modern and effective medical means—such as the pill and intrauterine devices—and thus has helped cut back unwanted pregnancies.

It's fashionable these days to criticize public programs—be they housing, education, health or whatever—and say they aren't working. From all we can tell, family-planning service for the needy *is* working. It is right on schedule and is producing results you can see. Let's hope that this program survives, and that millions of women will have the chance to take advantage of it, *if they want to.*

83

A few weeks ago the Supreme Court handed down a momentous decision on abortion. Basically, it said that most state laws on that subject are unconstitutional. And it opened the way for women to obtain abortions much more easily.

The Court decision drew a barrage of praise and damnation, for abortion is one of the most emotional, most delicate issues there is. And it has some special implications for the poor.

Last year more than a million American women underwent abortions to avoid having unwanted children. For a great many of them the experience was expensive, degrading and painful. For some, it was deadly. It's estimated that 500 to 1,000 American women have died each year as a result of complications from illegal abortions. Scores of thousands more were injured or became ill.

We've all heard some of the horror stories—about the teen-age girl who died after a real estate salesman, moonlighting as an abortionist, gave her four times too much anesthesia, or the woman who couldn't afford even a moonlighter, so she used a wire clothes hanger on herself.

Like so many other aspects of society, abortion has discriminated against the poor. Women with $200 or $2,000 could find a clean, safe clinic here in this country. Or they could fly to London or some other foreign city where abortion is out in the open. But the poor woman either risked doing the job on the kitchen table or sought out some dangerous back-alley hack.

Abortion laws in most states date back to the nineteenth century. And they never really prevented abortion; they just made it illegal. Estimates of the number of illegal abortions in the United States ranged from 200,000 to over one million per year.

But all that will be changing as a result of the Supreme Court ruling. The Court said that no state may interfere with a woman's right to get an abortion during the first three months of pregnancy. In the next three months, the state can intervene only to protect a mother's health by setting requirements about who can perform the abortion and where. The net effect will certainly be to make abortions much easier to obtain.

We already have some idea what the results of easier abortion will be. A study in states with liberal laws showed that when abortions are more readily available, they become safer and they are used more by blacks, poor and married women.

Three moral issues are interwoven in the difficult question of abortion. One involves the fetus—when does life begin? A second centers on the unwanted child, especially the child whose prospects for a dignified, happy life are not very good. And finally, there is the woman who feels her own well-being is threatened and sees abortion as an answer.

We are now free to weigh all of these concerns as we make *individual* decisions about abortion.

But the health of the black family does not always revolve around such weighty, controversial issues as contraception or abortion.

Not getting ripped off by innocent-looking vitamin peddlers may be of vital importance. Or just getting enough exercise—a very inexpensive "medicine"—may be all your family needs . . .

84

How many times since you were a child have you been urged to "Take your vitamins. They're good for you." Whatever the ill, we Americans take a pill.

We've been told that vitamins can cure sterility, impotence, diabetes, leg cramps, the common cold and a host of other ailments. As a result, the shelves at the corner drugstore are filled with everything from fruit-flavored baby vitamins to pills designed for the infirmities of old age.

Recently, however, we've begun to hear some warnings that vitamins are not a cure-all, and that overdoses can sometimes lead to trouble. The Food and Drug Administration—the FDA—has proposed a regulation to limit the level of vitamins A and D in nonprescription products. And a leading consumer organization contends that vitamin E supplements are a waste of money, at best.

The FDA says that too much vitamin A can cause headaches, irritability, increased pressure in the skull, dryness and cracking of skin and loss of appetite. And large doses have been known to retard growth in children.

As for vitamin D, large doses have been shown to retard the mental and physical growth of children and to cause hypertension and kidney failure.

The new regulation proposed by the FDA would deal mainly with multiple vitamin formulas. According to officials, some of these now contain sixty times the recommended daily allowance of vitamin D, and ten times the recommended dosage of vitamin A.

Vitamin E came under fire in a recent edition of *Consumer Reports*. An article said that the Consumers Union has not found any valid scientific evidence that vitamin E helps treat some sixty ailments. One exception—it does help a certain type of anemia in premature babies. Specifically, the article says vitamin E has not proven helpful in treating heart disease, as a number of its supporters claim.

Vitamin C is another which apparently can be overdone. Some doctors say large doses can cause kidney stones and upset sensitive stomachs.

Even if pills do not do any direct damage, they can indirectly hurt by leading patients to postpone proper medical treatment.

Nothing I've said is intended to imply that vitamins do not have any value and are not good for you—if they're taken in the right dosage. In general, doctors tell us that a balanced diet will provide all the vitamins the average person needs.

Unfortunately, millions of Americans don't get a balanced nutritional diet, for a variety of reasons, one of which is poverty. We should renew our efforts to see that such a diet is available to all.

85

Spring is here and that means it's time to pull out the old tennis racquet and head for the courts.

Time was, not very long ago, when you'd find precious few blacks, Puerto Ricans and other minorities or poor folk out on tennis courts. Tennis was pretty much a game played in white clothes by white people. Now and then an Arthur Ashe or Althea Gibson came along, but they were rare.

Things are changing. Tennis is moving out of the posh clubs. In fact, it's come to the streets of the ghettos.

If you'd been walking in Harlem on a Tuesday or Thursday morning last summer, you might have been startled as you came to 143rd Street and Seventh Avenue. There, stretched across the street, were a couple of tennis nets, and painted on the pavement were two tennis courts. Some thirty-five or forty kids, dressed in basketball shoes, jeans, sweat shirts, T-shirts or no shirts, were swatting tennis balls.

It was part of the "Tennis in the Streets" program sponsored by the Pepsi-Cola company. In three cities—New York, Philadelphia and Boston—mobile vans brought tennis to kids in the inner city. Courts were set up, racquets, balls and instruction provided free. Some twenty thousand youngsters took part, and this year several other cities will be added to bring tennis to thousands more.

Coca-Cola sponsors a national junior program in which boys and girls compete on tennis teams in twenty-four cities. Out of some fifty thousand who took part last year, it's estimated that 70 per cent were inner-city youths.

For a young black child, especially one from Harlem or North Philadelphia, tennis has been virtually an unknown sport. These kids have spent their summer days shooting baskets or playing stickball and dreaming of becoming another Wilt Chamberlain or Willie Mays.

Tennis offers a new form of fun and competition, and a new chance for athletic success and rewards. College scholarships are available for tennis players as well as for quarterbacks. Hundreds of jobs are opening at camps and clubs and parks for tennis teachers.

In addition, youngsters can learn something from these programs. One young boy—maybe twelve or thirteen years old—who showed up for the Harlem program was a trouble-maker and was stealing racquets and balls. As the weeks passed, he changed. He gave back the equipment he'd taken and became a leader in the project. As the director of a community tennis program puts it: "If kids are on tennis courts, then you know they're not in juvenile courts."

If you live in a city which has a community tennis program, get the word around to youngsters you know. If not, you might look into the possibility of getting one started. They're rewarding in a number of ways and can help break down one more old class barrier.

86

Pauline Betz Addie was women's tennis champion and undefeated professional way back in 1947. Which is to say she isn't eligible for this year's debutante outing. But she's still got the lean, healthy look that millions of young women might wish for. My wife, for that matter, is old enough to be married to your forty-nine-year-old commentator, and mother of his twenty-one- and twenty-year-old sons. But, thanks to tennis, she's still got the nice figure, good legs, a vitality that just plain disappears when women goof off and let themselves go.

If you want to stay healthy, and looking young, and

happy to be in the social swim of things, I've got a suggestion or two.

I don't know what you think is the fastest-growing indoor sport. Fussing with the spouse? Trying to outwit teenagers? Well, it's tennis, as Pauline Betz Addie tells us in her new book, *Tennis for Everyone.* I wish you women listeners would get Pauline's book, not just because she's a friend of mine, and not just because the Rowan household is full of tennis nuts.

You see, I like what's been happening to black women in the last four decades. No spindly legs, big hips, sagging breasts these days. Not among women who care. You see, black women are eating better. And that improved diet, plus better education and more pride, has improved the figures of black women immensely. Look around!

And don't you overlook what it does for the pride of black children to come home from school to a mother who is pretty, healthy, energetic. You may never hear your daughter say, "My mother is shapelier than your mother," or "My mother looks sexier than your mother," but you had better believe that they all want to think it. Well, neither your children nor your husband nor anyone else will say it if you're just hanging around the refrigerator or the bridge table.

Join the generation of *active* black women! And I can't think of an easier way to do it, leaving plenty of time to look out for your family, than to turn to tennis.

Pauline Betz Addie's book will give you a lot of tips for the beginner. Classes for learners are all over the place. Public courts go unused day after day in most cities. Fill them up!

I've been inspired to do this commentary because so many women I know have taken up tennis at ages of forty,

forty-seven, fifty-two. They're all having a ball, losing weight, finding new releases from the cares of the house or the job, finding new zip in their lives through tennis.

Try it. You'll like it. And somebody will like you a lot more.

We all know, though, that good health is hard to maintain where people do not have decent jobs —or where bigotry and corruption bar them from decent housing . . .

87

Among the few pluses of the Nixon Administration, where blacks are concerned, have been the Small Business Admininstration and the Office of Minority Business Enterprise, commonly known as OMBE. Between 1968 and late 1973 these two agencies made some $400 million worth of loans and grants to assist minority businessmen.

But now they are under fire. The Small Business Administration, which has made most of the loans, is facing special heat because probes in Richmond, Philadelphia and elsewhere have alleged bribery, corruption, other violations of law—and just plain maladministration.

I know—you're saying you've heard this song before. They created an Office of Economic Opportunity to aid the poor, but they took it away on grounds that crooks and deadbeats were taking the money. They had housing programs for the poor, but rich slick operators moved in on that, so now there are no meaningful housing programs for the poor.

Could it be that "Black Capitalism" was just a political farce, and that now they are going to take SBA and OMBE away from aspiring black businessmen on grounds of waste and corruption?

Well, two recent developments sure make the future look dim for OMBE and SBA. First, the General Accounting Office, the congressional watchdog agency, recently reported that just over half of all minority-owned business firms that have received federal aid have failed or are likely to fail soon. So the congressmen who appropriate the money already are being told that giving loans and grants to small black businesses is about like throwing dollars into a sinkhole.

Second, investigators are boring in on evidence that an awful lot of loans and grants have been given out to buy black political loyalty to President Nixon, with scant attention given to prospects of business success. Those of you who read my newspaper column will recall that during the 1972 presidential campaign I documented cases where small business loans were nothing more than political payoffs to black handkerchief heads.

Now black congressmen, like Representative Parren Mitchell of Maryland, and several legitimate black business groups are struggling to save OMBE and the SBA. Let us hope they succeed. Some black businesses are failing because discrimination has denied blacks the experience and know-how required for success. Taking away the small crumbs of opportunity thrown at them in recent years will not serve the national interest or the cause of justice.

And let it be clear that it was the White House, not black America, that put partisan politics into these programs.

The solution is to cleanse the OMBE and SBA of politics and corruption, tighten up the administration, and go on with the effort to give all Americans a piece of the free-enterprise pie.

88

A cruel irony is occurring in the wake of school desegregation in the South. As schools are integrated and more black children attend classes with whites, more black teachers and principals are losing their jobs or being demoted. Despite court orders to the contrary, in state after state the position, pay and prestige of black educators go down each time another school is desegregated.

It's not news that integration tends to dilute or destroy what is black by merging it with what is white. I've noted this often. Now some previously unpublished statistics from the Department of Health, Education and Welfare have been brought to light by the National Education Association and the Mississippi Teachers Association. They show just how bad things are.

In four Southern states—Alabama, Georgia, Louisiana and Mississippi, three fourths of the school districts show a drop of 2,500 black teachers between 1968, when meaningful integration started, and 1972. In the same period, the number of white teachers increased by over 3,400 in those districts.

In Florida, Georgia, Mississippi and Louisiana, almost 20 per cent of the school-principal jobs held by blacks were eliminated between 1968 and 1972. Meanwhile, white principalships increased 6 per cent.

Individual horror stories abound. In Georgia, a black man who had been a principal for twenty-five years found himself teaching social studies and history to seventh graders. In Alabama, a woman who had taught home economics for twenty-three years in an all-black school was assigned to teach second grade in an integrated school. Five days after she signed her new contract, she was fired for "incompetence."

Nobody is sure what happens to displaced black educators. Older ones often retire. The young may go to other school systems or take jobs in industry and govenrment. But we do know that the effects of this on youngsters and communities can be traumatic.

For a long time, the best black college graduates went into the field of education. It was one of the few professions that offered talented blacks a chance for work and advancement. At the same time, it gave black youngsters a set of black men and women whom they could look up to—something they desperately needed.

Now, as black educators are transferred and demoted, they're often no longer able to serve as examples or leaders. And their communities, especially the young people in those communities, are the losers.

That is a steep price indeed—and an unwarranted one—for blacks to have to pay for school integration.

89

Organized labor is in some kind of mess these days. It is run by overfat, oversoft suburban dwellers who can't quite keep up with the pretense that they are the saviors of the wretched working class. Labor leaders in the nation's capital have taken an unquenchable liking to playing golf at the Burning Tree Country Club, even though they can't stomach the insinuation that they have gone conservative, even Republican. Labor leaders have seen so much money flowing loose in banks that they control, pension funds that they administer, strike funds that they manipulate, that they have begun to spend more time figuring out how to shaft one another, or even murder each other, than how to combat what used to be the greedy capitalist opposition.

Antilabor I am not. I still belong to a variety of unions, at considerable cost, some of which I could have abandoned long ago. I belong out of the conviction that organized labor in its best days helped to make American capitalism an honorable system, helped to do in the robber barons and make the American workingman the most affluent workingman in the world.

I have stayed in some unions, also, because organized labor for years was a powerful force for racial justice. The Newspaper Guild has done a lot to make reporting something other than a Jim Crow exercise. AFTRA has had its impact on radio and television. The United Auto Workers and the late Walter Reuther were tremendous forces for decency in this society.

Yet, it is undeniable that organized labor is not what it used to be. AFL-CIO President George Meany played footsie with President Nixon during the 1972 presidential election campaign, mostly because of personal pique with George McGovern, and now Meany cries like a baby every time Mr. Nixon announces a policy he doesn't like. A former member of the Painters Union, Peter J. Brennan, is Secretary of Labor, but Labor regards him as a traitor because when the big chips go down, Brennan always seems to go along with the Administration.

The painters, carpenters, bricklayers and all the other craft unions would like to hate this Administration. But the craft unions also like to keep blacks and Puerto Ricans and Indians and anyone but their relatives out of their juicy work scheme. And since the Nixon Administration has stopped making noises about a "Philadelphia Plan" and a "Chicago Plan" or any other plan to require a certain percentage of minority workers, the craft unions aren't complaining too vociferously about Mr. Nixon.

Yet, Meany is mad enough not to invite the President to the AFL-CIO's Biennial Convention in Bal Harbour, Florida. And he didn't send Brennan the traditional invitation. And when Mr. Nixon vetoed the minimum-wage bill in September 1973, Meany proclaimed that Mr. Nixon would go down in history as "one of our poorest Presidents."

But the unforgettable fact is that union leaders and workers helped elect Mr. Nixon with an overwhelming mandate. And in doing so they revealed both racism and a *nouveau*-prosperous snobbishness. In doing so, labor unions were playing a game that was self-destructive.

Does angry George Meany now know that he can't play it both ways? I doubt it.

90

Every month we hear figures on how many Americans are employed and unemployed. Lately, in early 1973, unemployment has been running around 5 or 6 per cent, or 4,400,000 to 5,500,000 persons.

That's bad enough. But it represents just the tip of an iceberg. In our big cities, millions more are *under*employed, which means that even though they have jobs, they don't earn enough to live decently.

These are the working poor—porters, cleaning ladies, clerks, night watchmen, dishwashers, clothes pressers and dozens of others. Often a high percentage is black. Their plight is not just a personal tragedy. It strikes at the very heart of the ills which trouble our cities.

As part of the 1970 census a survey was made of fifty-one inner-city areas . . . areas which are about 50 per cent black. It was found that more than half the workers did not earn enough money to maintain decent standards of living for their families, and that 30 per cent did not even earn poverty-level incomes of about $4,000 a year.

These figures include the unemployed. But they include others, too. Those who've become so discouraged that they've quit looking for jobs. Those who work part-time and can't find full-time work.

These are not people who have opted out of the labor force for good. They are people who work a good deal of the time and don't just sit home waiting for a welfare check.

What happens when a family doesn't earn enough to live

decently? It breaks up, and welfare rolls swell. It cannot care for homes and apartments, so eventually buildings decay, and this rot spreads to whole neighborhoods. Desperate men turn to alcohol and drugs to forget, or to crime to earn a little more money to pay the bills.

What happens, in short, is that we create the crisis of our cities.

It is not laziness that is at the heart of our urban ills. Not innate immoralty or hereditary lack of brains. It is poverty. Poverty not just of the *un*employed, but of vast hordes of *under*employed.

What can be done about underemployment that's crippling so many individuals and communities? Income redistribution is one answer. Another is programs which would put people to work on public-service jobs . . . teachers' aides, health workers and the like. And a higher minimum wage certainly would help.

Full employment at decent wages is not just a sop for the poor. The federal government loses an estimated $12 billion to $15 billion a year in taxes for each 1 per cent of unemployment. If you add in all the underemployed, the loss is staggering. And it is a loss that is borne by us all.

91

It used to be that when Johnny came marching home, we met him with bands, parades and a hero's welcome.

Nowadays, when Johnny comes straggling home from Vietnam, he often finds himself ignored or even scorned, jobless, disillusioned and unable to cope with civilian life. And no veteran knows these troubles better than the black one.

Since 1964, over 7 million servicemen have returned to civilian life, including more than 3 million who served in Asia. For many, it's been a wrenching, discouraging experience.

Listen to what a black ex-Marine from Chicago told a reporter from *Ebony* magazine: "I'm worse off now than I was when I left. Two whole years in the service, down the drain . . . It's strange, but after a while you sort of get to the point where you don't really give a damn."

A Senate subcommittee which investigated the plight of Viet veterans was told that a climate of ignorance, apathy and indifference prevails in this country where veterans are concerned. Partly this is due to the unpopularity of the Vietnam war. It did not inspire a sense of purpose in many servicemen and did not earn them respect at home.

The problems and frustrations of veterans are many. At the top of the list is getting work. The unemployment rate among vets in their twenties has run about 50 per cent higher than for the rest of the nation. For blacks, it's three times higher. There have been periods when one out of every four or five young black veterans was without a job.

Emotional problems are common, too. It's not easy to come home and pick up where you left off. In this respect, too, minorities and poor feel the pressure even more because their behavior often goes unnoticed and help is not as readily available.

What can be done to aid our ex-GIs?

One thing is to expand and coordinate efforts to get jobs for them. There are lots of programs, both government and private, but critics say that they are too fragmented.

We can also make it easier for the veteran to go back to school. Take another look at the GI Bill, which pays only a fraction of today's steep college costs. Colleges should set up special projects to prepare vets for school and give them leeway to design their own programs.

What has happened to many veterans is tragic, especially in black communities, for the veteran represents a special kind of hope there. He brings back new skills and leadership experience, and he could be a constructive influence. But he needs and deserves help if he is to realize this potential.

92

At least nine out of ten men and women who are sent to prison will come out someday—most of them within two or three years. But what happens when they do is discouraging and dangerous, both to them and to society. These men and women will find that it's awfully hard to get a job. Black ex-convicts, in particular, will have a tough time.

As a result, large numbers of former inmates—perhaps as many as three out of four—wind up committing new crimes and being sent back to jail. Out of desperation and necessity, crime becomes a means of survival for them, the only way they find for getting money.

Why do prison inmates have such a hard time finding work after they're released? For one thing, if they're black—and many are—they've never had much of a chance for a decent education. They may not have graduated from high school, and as a result, they can't get decent-paying jobs. When competing for menial work, they often run into racial discrimination.

Another reason it's so hard to find work is that many offenders have spent a good part of their lives in jail. This means they have no usable job experience.

A third factor is that they don't receive adequate preparation in prison for getting and holding a job on the outside. Often the vocational programs in penal institutions are geared to the needs of the institution, not the individuals. Many prisoners spend their working hours making license plates or picking cotton. And there's not much demand for license-plate makers outside the prison walls.

Finally, a major factor in the difficulty of getting jobs is the fear which society has about hiring former offenders. They are considered dangerous, untrustworthy, violent. In many states anyone convicted of a felony automatically is barred from any job which requires a license, such as barber, beautician or ambulance driver.

What can be done to change the situation?

To start with, our penal institutions can offer more worthwhile, useful job training to inmates—teach them skills that will be relevant once they're released. But it's not enough just to teach a vocation. We must help reorient and remotivate offenders, give them more responsibility over their lives so they can function normally in society.

And finally, the public must be willing to accept ex-cons and make jobs available to them. We should loosen some of the tight restrictions on hiring these men and give them a chance.

In the end, society, as well as those individuals, will

benefit from that kind of approach. The rationale behind carefully regulating jobs and keeping ex-prisoners from holding them is to shield and protect the public. But in fact, an angry ex-prisoner who cannot find a job presents far greater danger than one who is working and earning a living.

If job discrimination has been a grim burden for black Americans, housing discrimination has been a special prison.

Whites who under the pressure of law would tolerate a token number of black workers in their midst worked overtime to ensure that no black families moved into their neighborhoods.

Sometimes they were motivated by economic fears—the old notion that property values drop whenever blacks move in. In some instances, sexual fears dominated. Whites sensed that interracial sex and marriage have become more commonplace in America. Housing separation is still viewed as a primary barrier to "mongrelization."

In other instances, nothing more venal than snobbery was at issue. It is still considered a measure of social and economic prestige by some Americans to be able to say, "There are no blacks or Jews in our community . . ."

93

A man's home is his castle—so the old saying tells us. Unfortunately, millions of blacks and other minority groups often must be content with standing on the other side of the moat and admiring someone else's castle.

For a long time there have been significant gaps in the housing patterns of blacks and whites. A new analysis by the Census Bureau indicates that housing for all Americans improved considerably in the 1960s, but that blacks still are lagging.

During the 1960s, increasing numbers of Americans lived in homes which were less crowded and which contained more of the amenities of life—things like bathrooms, air conditioning, washing machines, freezers.

The Census Bureau says a crowded home is one in which there is more than one person per room. Using that standard, about 20 per cent of American homes were crowded in 1940, but only 8 per cent in 1970. During the twenty years between 1950 and 1970, the number of homes with all normal plumbing facilities increased from 66 to 94 per cent. Black families registered dramatic gains: 83 per cent had full plumbing in 1970, compared with 30 per cent in 1950.

That is the good news as far as blacks are concerned. Here's the bleaker part of the picture.

In 1970, 65 per cent of white families owned the homes they lived in. Among blacks, only 42 per cent owned their own homes. Although the percentage of homeowners in both races increased during the 1960s, the gap between blacks and whites remained just about the same as it was twenty and thirty years ago.

The Census report also shows that black families are more likely to live in older housing. Forty-nine per cent occupied dwellings built before 1939, compared with 40 per cent of all American families.

There's a substantial housing shortage in America today. This scarcity affects all classes and all races, but none so much as the poor, especially poor blacks. Middle- and upper-income whites can postpone their dream of home-ownership, and find comfortable places to rent. Eventually they can buy a home in the suburbs. But low-income persons often are trapped in decayed or decaying cities or remote rural areas.

That is why it is so important that our public officials face up to the situation, and to the housing needs of low-income families. Everyone deserves the chance to feel that *his* home is *indeed* a castle.

94

One of the great American dreams is to own your own home. Blacks dream bigger dreams than most Americans, because they are among the poorest-housed people in the land. But white-collar crooks have been turning their dreams into nightmares.

Over the last forty years the federal government has increasingly recognized the ugly truth that millions of Americans are ill-housed. So we now have federally financed public housing, federal subsidies to buyers and renters, FHA and VA guarantees of mortgages.

But this success has been tarnished by some incredible frauds by fast-buck artists who have turned help-the-poor programs into rook-the-poor schemes. On top of this, there has been mismanagement, negligence, hasty legislation that cost taxpayers hundreds of millions of dollars. Giant public housing projects stand vacant and vandalized, as in St. Louis. The government winds up owning thousands of wretched houses that poor victims were tricked into buying and then couldn't pay for, as in Detroit.

This is how it works. And if you dream of owning *your* own house, you'd better listen closely. A speculator goes into a neighborhood where the first black family has bought. He scares the devil out of the other white families, causing them to sell and run, getting a price far below the real value of their property. The speculator makes a few inexpensive repairs and then gets a grossly inflated FHA appraisal of the house, sometimes by bribing the appraiser. The speculator finds a not-well-educated black buyer whom he might even convince to lie about his job and his income in order to get a huge FHA-insured mortgage approved.

The dreamy buyer moves in. He quickly discovers the house needs major repairs he did not expect and cannot afford. The mortgage payments and utility bills are too big for his meager salary.

The buyer falls behind in his payments, eventually defaults, and the government must pay his mortgage and take the house. The fast-buck artist is richer, the taxpayers are poorer—and the poor fellow who dreamed of owning his own home is in debt, and deeply disillusioned.

There is a lesson in this for people eager to own a home.

Don't deal with anyone who asks you to lie about your job or income so you can get a mortgage. If you are poorly informed about home buying, as most people are, spend a few dollars for good legal or other advice.

95

In American race relations, interracial marriage and the busing of schoolchildren are probably the most emotional issues, but surely, not far behind is the matter of integrated housing. Talk about a black family moving into an all-white area, and some whites are quickly whipped into a violent mood over the prospect of their property values dropping.

Even blacks and white liberals have sort of taken it as a truism that when a neighborhood becomes integrated, the grass dies automatically, the paint peels, potholes pop up in the streets like magic, crime arrives with the sunset, and everybody loses money.

Well, won't they all be surprised to read the headline article in the November issue of *Money* magazine! It says: "IT PAYS TO STAY WHEN BLACKS MOVE IN." The article provides convincing evidence that "Contrary to a pernicious myth, property values in integrated areas usually keep pace with those in white areas—and sometimes rise faster."

Everyone has heard about the old blockbusting techniques. A black family moves into an all-white area. A real estate agent then runs through the white neighborhood, shouting, "The niggers are coming," and panicky whites sell him their properties at absurdly low prices. The agent then sells the property to blacks at ridiculously high prices. After which the fleeing whites tell friends and relatives how one black family moved in "and we lost $5,000 on the sale of our house."

The *Money* article makes it clear that this kind of racial madness still occurs. Thus, there aren't many neighborhoods in this country where blacks and whites live together easily, maintaining a racial balance. But the article in *Money* documents conclusively that where whites do not panic, property values rise handily in integrated neighborhoods.

In the Shaker Heights area of Cleveland, which is about 33 per cent black, a house that sold for $29,000 in 1970 went for $33,500 in July 1973. That is an appreciation of 4.9 per cent a year. In the 99 per cent white suburb of University Heights, a house that sold for $29,000 in 1970 went for $34,000 in March 1973. That is a gain of 5.8 per cent per year.

In the Seattle area, a house in an area that is 36 per cent black showed a price rise of $10,850 between 1968 and 1973, whereas a house in the virtually all-white Laurelhurst area increased in value by only $4,500. The house in the integrated area appreciated at three times the rate of the house in the lily-white area.

If you are concerned about housing—and every black family ought to be—get a copy of *Money* and read the whole article. Black people can stand to have some myths destroyed, too.

Part V

Black Perspectives on the Future

By the time you hold a copy of this book, the black perspective on many issues with which I have dealt may have changed drastically.

Richard Nixon may have yielded the Presidency to Gerald Ford of Michigan. That would not change the political or ideological philosophy in the White House to any appreciable degree, for we have noted that on the crucial issues before the Congress when Ford was in the House, only one congressman voted more loyally for President Nixon's position than Ford: Representative Barber Conable, Jr., of New York.

Yet it would be unfair to even suggest that with Ford as President the outlook for blacks would not change substantially. Ford already has gone out of his way to establish a dialogue with blacks, something Nixon seemed deliberately to avoid. To put it bluntly, Ford would bring a higher level of racial decency to the White House. He surely would not surround himself with key advisers who have infused the government with the not-so-subtle racism that has been a hallmark of the last six years.

Yet, by the time you read this, Richard Nixon may have survived impeachment efforts, and only the passage of time, of "two more years," will offer blacks any meaningful perspective of hope.

No matter how the political cards fall, we know that many new difficulties are ahead. They flow out of the "energy crisis" and the other woes of the economy. But we also see harbingers of better times to come.

The educational outlook has become cloudy . . .

96

During the past sixteen months I've reported to you proudly about the upsurge in the number of blacks going on to higher education. Well, today I've got a bit of bad news. A nationwide survey shows that the number of blacks who enrolled as freshmen in colleges in the fall of 1973 was down sharply from the fall of 1972.

Black enrollment was up to 8.7 per cent in 1972, a figure reasonably approaching the black ratio of the population, which is 11 per cent. But all of a sudden in the 1973–74 school year, black enrollment dropped to 7.8 per cent. And the reasons why may be more disturbing than the figures themselves.

It might not be so surprising if I told you that fewer blacks are enrolling in the prestigious, high-tuition colleges and universities. That you might expect, considering higher unemployment and prices and the general state of the economy. But a survey by Alexander Astin for the American Council on Education and UCLA shows that enrollment of blacks and other minorities has declined at every *kind* of institution: the two-year college, the four-year public college, the four-year private college, the universities.

That means the killing of the dream for many a black youngster. And every time an ambitious black youngster fails to go on to greater learning, it means more years of second-class citizenship, not just for that black teen-ager but perhaps thousands more.

Why the sudden drop in black enrollment? We have to face the fact that many thousands of black students have gone to college in recent years because someone other than his family furnished financial assistance. Most colleges just don't have the money for scholarships and other assistance that they used to have. And those that still have money have shifted their priorities away from aiding blacks, Chicanos, Indians and other minorities.

Part of the problem is that the energy crisis, impeachment, food prices, women's rights, ecology are at the center of interest of most Americans these days. But there is also something of a white backlash involved. Middle-class parents have been screaming that only the very rich and the very poor—especially the minority poor—can now afford to go to college. So a lot of schools that once thought it just and decent to give a single black student $4,000 a year in aid have now decided it is more politic to give $1,000 a year to four white students who are not quite so needy—but whose parents are more vocal than are those of the poor black students.

It seems clear that if blacks are to continue to make

great strides in college education, blacks will have to do more to help themselves—and each other.

97

We've all heard of dropouts. And cop-outs. Well, here's a new addition to your vocabulary: push-out. And it's a word that has special meaning for blacks.

Push-outs are young people who have been expelled or suspended from school, or who finally quit because they can't stand all the hostility directed against them. They're students who are "pushed out" of school by discriminatory treatment, or who get so upset by the hostile environment that they leave on their own.

A great many of the push-outs are blacks who are victims of racial discrimination and arbitrary acts on the part of school authorities. Their story has been dramatically told in a report prepared by the Southern Regional Council and the Robert F. Kennedy Memorial.

School desegregation has proceeded slowly enough in this country. And even when it has occurred, continued resistance has made life difficult for blacks, Chicanos, Indians and other minorities.

Often they've been excluded from extracurricular activities, been met with hostility and condescension, or been singled out for disciplinary action. In the South, confrontations are provoked with black students by the use of symbols like the Confederate flag, or by the displacement of black principals, teachers and coaches. The fear of biracial dating has been used to justify disciplinary action for innocent greetings between black and white students. Curriculums continue to be geared to white, middle-class college-bound students, thereby discouraging blacks.

This doesn't mean school desegregation is failing. Rather, it's unending resistance to desegregation—by some teachers, administrators, government officials and others—that creates the climate for the great number of push-outs.

How serious is the problem? A nationwide survey in 1970–71 showed that the expulsion rate for minority students was twice that for nonminorities, and the expulsion rate for black students was three times that for nonminority students.

Whenever a minority student is pushed out of school this way, both the youngster and society suffer—in terms of pride, future potential, loss of a better citizen. Look at earning power alone: a black male who graduates from high school would earn an average of $76,000 more over his lifetime than one who did not get through the twelfth grade.

The problem of push-outs can be combated on several fronts—from local school districts to the federal government. But most important, according to the report, is that all school districts which are desegregating give students a meaningful role in planning and carrying out the desegregation programs. For school integration has been most sucessful—and the push-out problem the lowest—when students were genuinely involved from the start.

As the report on push-outs notes: "There is no better place to help students prepare for responsible roles in our democracy than as active participants in the quest for equal educational opportunity."

Yet even as the educational outlook grew murky, a new degree of hope was springing up in the field of criminal justice.

98

Most of us do our best to stay as far away as we can from police and courts and the whole system of criminal justice.

Chances are that if you've ever come in contact with that system, you've had a bad experience. You've been hassled or ignored; you've become angry and frustrated. That's true for little things, like traffic tickets. It's true even if you've only been a witness. And it's especially true if you're a member of a minority group.

For a long time, efforts to improve the criminal-law system concentrated on police and prisons. Now there's a move to focus on a new area—the individual citizens. Get them involved, treat them better, make the system responsive to their needs.

In January 1974 Donald Santarelli, administrator of the Law Enforcement Assistance Administration, made an important speech. In it, he called for concentrating on a new citizens' program in the criminal-justice system.

Santarelli noted the sour taste most of us have if we ever have anything to do with the law. Most of us who've been stopped and given a ticket are angered, not because we think we're innocent, but because we're treated in a demeaning way by policemen. And it doesn't stop there. If you go

into court with the case, you often face endless delays, waiting, postponements.

Or consider the victims and witnesses in criminal cases.
One of the major reasons offenders go free is that witnesses
don't cooperate, and one of the main reasons they don't is
that they're afraid of what might happen if they talk. They
are not adequately protected. Nor is the whole system explained to them so they know what's happening.

In the same way, a lot of people don't report crimes
because they don't think the police will do anything about
them, or because they're afraid they'll get trapped in a
maze of procedures and legal gobbledegook—or worse yet,
be ignored.

Santarelli admits things are particularly bad when it
comes to minorities. He acknowledges that police-community
relations programs have little substance or relation to reality.

Says Santarelli: "We have to tear down the walls that
separate the residents of inner cities from their fellow citizens. Where the walls cannot yet be torn down, then we
have to build bridges. The dissension, the isolation, the suspicion must be overcome—with programs that protect and
serve the people."

There are many ideas for increasing citizen participation in law enforcement: community-relations bureaus and
civilian review boards for police, courts and other agencies;
a central complaint bureau; reports by police to victims on
how the investigation and handling of their case is going.
Even technical things, like building courtrooms so that
everyone can hear what's being said.

Take the case of witnesses. A lot of people don't report
crimes because they have to wait, or they're shunted off

or badgered. Police departments should make it easy for citizens to report crime and get effective action. Ways must be found to protect witnesses so they will come forward willingly.

Or jurors. If you've ever been called for jury duty, you know that half the time usually is spent in a dingy waiting room. If nothing else, we can at least make the jurors' room livable.

The inconveniences of the court system are illustrated in a story told by Supreme Court Justice Byron White. He says that he went for a dental appointment one day and found twenty-five patients in the waiting room. Six hours later, when he finally was in the dentist's chair, he asked what the problem was.

The dentist replied that he had gone to court a few days before. He was told to be there at 9 A.M.—along with fifty or sixty other people. But his case wasn't called until 3 P.M. If that's the right way to run a court, the dentist reasoned, it's the right way to run a dental office. So now he tells all patients to arrive at 9 A.M. It may not be convenient for them, but like the judge, it's great for the dentist.

The moral of this is that our criminal-justice system has been operated too long for the benefit of prosecutors, judges, attorneys—not for victims, witnesses, jurors.

That must be changed. As Santarelli says: "The system cannot continue following the course of ignoring or abusing the very citizens it was originally designed to serve."

99

Like everyone else in America, you've noticed the sharp increase of black mayors of America's cities, and the soaring numbers of other black elected officials. But something of equal or even greater importance has been happening that you may have overlooked. Whereas there were only a few black judges a generation ago, some 325 blacks sit on the bench today, dispensing justice to blacks and whites alike.

This has increased trust and hope among black people, and it has created uneasiness among some whites who think a black judge is automatically "soft on crime." A few whites already are clamoring for legal changes in our system of justice so as to dilute the influence of black judges and jurors.

Blacks still make up only 2 to 3 per cent of the judges in this country, but the power of black judges is greater than the percentages indicate, for almost all the black judges are in densely populated cities. Thus a white person in trouble with the law in Detroit, Washington, D.C., Philadelphia, has about a 50-50 chance of facing a black judge. This terrifies some whites who seem to fear that blacks will "get even" for the generations during which many white judges gave blacks a raw deal.

Dwight Chapin, President Nixon's former appointments secretary, recently tried to get his perjury trial moved out of Washington, D.C., on grounds that he couldn't get a fair verdict from a black jury. Chapin argued that some of the "dirty tricks" linked to him during the 1972 presidential campaign were directed against blacks and that knowledge of this would prejudice the jury. The courts refused to move the trial.

But that doesn't mean that whites have ceased to be nervous about black judges. They seem to think that black jurists automatically are civil libertarians who are soft on crime, especially black crime. Let a black judge follow a liberal bail policy, as does Judge Bruce Wright of New York City, and the press is quick to pin on a derogatory label such as "cut-'em-loose Bruce."

The truth is that black judges are less inclined to take a policeman's word automatically. Black judges know how quick policemen are to haul in a black teen-ager who just seemed "uppity." They know of too many cases where policemen lied or manufactured evidence. So they honor constitutional protections, especially for first offenders. Yet when it comes to violent crime, black judges don't buy the old racist notion that "it's just two black boys cutting each other up, so give 'em a slap on the wrist."

This reporter's observation is that black judges are just like white judges. They come in all shapes, sizes, intellects, ambitions, egos and degrees of compassion.

May it always be so.

Still, the elections of more black mayors and other officials, the appointments of more black judges, have not erased black anxiety . . .

100

Wherever I meet with blacks these days, especially young blacks, the inevitable question is whether blacks have a decent future in this society. They refer to unyielding job discrimination, lingering abuses in housing, the vicelike grip of poverty, hostility and bigotry in all things social, and many of them seem on the verge of despair.

I make it clear that the future will be rough, especially the years immediately ahead. But I also make it clear that we black Americans are not without hope.

Some cynicism on the part of blacks is healthy. Too many times in the past we have celebrated what we thought were lasting victories, only to have our dreams shattered. In the Reconstruction period following the Civil War, blacks who were thrust into positions of power no doubt thought they had achieved lasting roles in the political life of the Deep South. They soon were back in bondage.

When the Supreme Court outlawed racial segregation in public schools in 1954, millions of us rejoiced at the thought that Jim Crow was dead. We know, sadly, what a tough, tricky old bird he is.

During the demonstrations of the late fifties, the great civil rights march of 1963, some blacks truly believed their chant, "We shall overcome . . ."

Now years of fighting hard just to stand still have made it clear to us that the price of our liberation must be constant struggle and eternal vigilance.

Perhaps nothing is a more pointed commentary on the

feeble magnitude of black participation in their federal government than the gallery of photographs that was spread across the front pages of most newspapers on March 2, 1974. A grand jury had indicted seven of the most powerful former members of the Nixon Administration on charges of conspiring to cover up the Watergate crimes—and every man indicted was white. In fact, more than forty people in government and industry had pleaded guilty, been convicted, paid fines or been indicted in the most sensational political scandal in American history. Not one was black. The only black involved in the whole mess was former Watergate night watchman Frank Wills, who tripped up the burglars and opened up to public scrutiny what former Attorney General John Mitchell called "the White House horrors."

Now, some would call it racial progress had the power grabbers included a few blacks among the plotters, schemers, burglarizers. But I regard it as racial progress that this overweeningly powerful, lily-white group, with all its appeals to racism and snobbery, could not completely bamboozle the American people.

If we black people develop some new goals that we can share; if we help each other to seize educational and employment opportunities; if we discard slovenly indifference and move with pride, to use the tools and powers that we have, we shall yet find an army of white allies.

And we shall breathe new life into the old dream that "We shall overcome."

About the Author

CARL T. ROWAN is the only newspaperman to win the coveted Sigma Delta Chi medallion three years in succession—twice for foreign correspondence and once for his reporting of national affairs.

In 1961, after thirteen years as correspondent for the Minneapolis *Tribune*, he joined the Kennedy Administration as Deputy Assistant Secretary of State. President Kennedy later named him to the U.S. Delegation to the United Nations, then Ambassador to Finland, where he became the youngest American envoy in the world. After some time abroad, President Johnson recalled him from Finland to replace the ailing Edward R. Murrow as Director of the U.S. Information Agency.

After four and a half years of public service, Carl Rowan returned to journalism in 1965 as an internationally syndicated columnist for the Chicago *Daily News*. In addition to the commentaries from his "Black Perspectives" radio broadcasts that form the nucleus of this book, he is a regular commentator on political and social events for the radio and television stations of Post-Newsweek Broadcasting. He is also a roving editor for *Reader's Digest*.

Mr. Rowan, his wife and their three children live in Washington, D.C.